The Art of Being a Woman

ALEXANDRA ADOMAITIS

Copyright © 2017 by Alexandra Adomaitis
All rights reserved. This book or any portion thereof
may not be reproduced or used in any manner whatsoever
without the express written permission of the publisher
except for the use of brief quotations in a book review.

Printed in the United States of America

First Printing, 2017

ISBN 978-0-9990203-1-9

Los Angeles, CA

www.alexandratheartist.com

This book is dedicated to all of the Queens who wear their crowns with pride, and care for their people with love and strength.

CONTENTS

Foreword vii
Preface ix

La Femme | *xi*

Essence Of A Goddess | *1*

Chapter One: Body By… You! 3
Chapter Two: Miss Manners. 21
Chapter Three: Loyalty. 33
Chapter Four: Can You Relate? 39
Chapter Five: Nothing Compares 2 U 63
Chapter Six: Self Defense & Self-Respect 73

Gilding The Lily | *83*

Chapter Seven: Scent Of A Woman 85
Chapter Eight: Hey Good Lookin' .95
Chapter Nine: La Cocina. 115
Chapter Ten: ~~Bitch Better~~ ~~Have My~~ Make Her Own Money . .131
Chapter Eleven: Women Of Inspiration 145

Final Musings | *159*

In Conclusion 165
Acknowledgement 167
Bibliography. 169

FOREWORD

"There are no ugly women in the world, just lazy ones." This quote is attributed variously to Coco Chanel, Estee Lauder and Helena Rubinstein. It's a quip with only a ring of truth to it. There is an extended version attributed to Diana Polska: "There are no ugly women, there are only women who don't know how to look pretty." And that is a slight mutation of a quote that I read, as a child, in a little book called "Women, Heroes and a Frog," which has stuck with me from the moment it seared itself into my youngster brain: "There are no ugly women, there are only women who don't know how to look beautiful."

And there you have it. It's that one word that makes the difference. But what everyone, everywhere always, always… always… forgets, or discards, or discounts, is that "beautiful" is an inside job. Just as all art begins as an inside job… so does the art of being a woman. Beautiful on the inside… hell, you could wear burlap down Rodeo

Drive, head held high, and the next day, burlap might just be fabric of the moment. It's all attitude. Alexandra Adomaitis is our new best friend forever (no acronyms here, thank you) as she plumbs with a relentless spirit of not quite, but almost servitude in her quest for what makes women works of art in all of art's manifestations.

The women who were courageous enough to answer her questions cover the map of the women-only world… they are the painters, sculptors, gardeners, alchemists and wizards. These women spin straw into gold, sometimes to wear, sometimes only to buy more straw. But it's all an art. Hope, wonder and delight smash cut with fear, brutality, and the utter messes we women can make of our days and lives, only to rise as a masterpiece every morning. Being a woman has never been easy. Even in these increasingly profound enlightened ages, women are still questioned, demeaned and often treated like second-class citizens. Yet, despite the struggles women continue to face, we do it with panache, grace, humor and style. We are fierce and deserve everything we work for. What is the art of being a woman? You'll have a better idea at the end of the book.

-Carolyn Hennesy

PREFACE

Welcome to what I felt was only appropriate to entitle "The Art of Being a Woman." A book I've had so much fun writing, and am very pleased to share it with you now. I am not a beauty blogger, nor am I a therapist or health guru. I'm a complicated young woman who grew up a dancer, and became an artist entrepreneur of sorts. I have not made my millions yet, or married the man of my dreams, so why did I write this book, you might ask. What makes Alexandra so qualified to tell women how it is, or dictate their life choices? While I may not be Tony Robbins or Oprah, I do hope that this book prompts discussions all around. I don't want to tell you how to live your life, I just want those reading this book to gain insight from a variety of women on how to find and better your own badass self.

I'm a constant work in progress, an evolving woman, if you will, with a closet full of issues and heartache. I also have a life filled with incredible achievements, and a lot to be happy and grateful for. In this book, I've compiled a wide range of material, ideas and tips from other women, years of research and, of course, my own opinions. Before you delve any deeper into this fabulous lexicon of do's and don'ts, I want to make it known that I am a female who tells it like it is.

Some genius person somewhere on the internet once said, "I don't sugarcoat shit, I'm not Willy Wonka," and I said "Amen!" Not everyone may agree with me and not everyone likes me, but that's fine because opinions are like assholes, everybody has one. (A big thank you to Trish for that amazing line.) I am by no means the perfect woman (which doesn't exist), but I do appreciate well-rounded, amazing females that continue to surprise, entertain and work the life they have laid out for themselves. While creating this book, I interviewed multitudes of women from a variety of backgrounds, ages and ethnicities. We discussed and shared our individual stories and opinions about the feminine identity, and my discoveries were fascinating. I spent a lot of time thinking about what was truly important to share with the women (and men) who would be reading this book. So, please enjoy and utilize it to its fullest. Know that you are not alone and you are a beautiful female. There are billions of women around the world - every one of us different, every one of us a stunning expression, capable of powerful beauty and immense soul.

La Femme

No matter how difficult things may get, I am grateful every day of my life that I am indeed a woman. Women for centuries have been repressed, constrained and generally dismissed by a male-driven society, yet we survive. We thrive, we adapt and we continue to push boundaries laid out for us thousands of years prior to today's existence. Whether you're a tender nurturer, a fierce brazen individual, or somewhere in between, all women are strong emotional creatures that can never be replaced. We are the backbone and behind the scenes champions to successful men throughout history. We are the mothers, daughters and sisters of revolution, as we continue writing our own history in this world and struggle for our place at the table of equality. So much is expected of us and yet, the credit that is due is rarely given. Though men may have their ideas of what a woman is, we live it every day - the good, the bad and everything in between. Some of us are given everything at birth, while others make their own gilded lives, but only we as women get to experience the magic and illumination that is, the art of being a woman.

Though I was shy throughout my childhood, I've grown into an independent, strong-willed woman who (for the most part) can take care of herself. One of my setbacks, for example, is that I *still* can't change my car's oil, much to my father's chagrin. But hey, you can't win 'em all! I did, however, grow up with the knowledge that I never need a man's validation to have self-worth, and to this day, I still know that deep in my core. The very idea of any man telling me what to do and how to do it is simply hilarious.

On the flip side to that comment, I don't aim to disempower the opposite sex. I love men! (Especially when they have yummy biceps. Delicious!) Men are our counterpart, and the balance to our very being. In my mind, I don't feel one sex could exist without the other, but on that note, I have a story…

Once upon a time, on planet Earth, I actually had a *man-child* (I use this title for a male over a certain age that cannot get his shit together nor does he respect women) look me straight in the eye and tell me that several years from now, women would become obsolete and go extinct. His "scientific" reasoning for this laughable and unrealistic projection was that female robots would have replaced us, and would be able to do all the tasks women used to perform, including all sexual acts, mind you. When this robot takeover occurs, men wouldn't need women for anything, and would kill them all off. He felt that, in the meantime of waiting for this inevitability, men should be able to do whatever they wanted to do to women, whenever. He used much more colorful and vulgar terms when he spoke, but let that sink in for a second… this is a true story, I kid you not. Oh, AND he shared these "facts" with an audience that included his then girlfriend. #Classy.

I was so stunned by everything this man-child was practically yelling into my face, that I couldn't find a reaction other than to laugh. Aside from the blatant misogyny and disgusting rhetoric, the very idea of men existing on this planet without women is ridiculous. Men and women balance each other out; one sex is not greater than the other. Also, why the murdering? That was the one part I definitely could not figure out, but in my head, I couldn't stop repeating, "run, bitch" to his then girlfriend.

Throughout the years, I have met more and more females who've lost the very idea of what it means to be a woman. Now, the definition of "being a true woman" will vary immensely depending on whom you talk to, and what they have been brought up to believe; there cannot be one correct answer. However, one of the main reasons I chose to write this book is because I feel that multitudes of women have lost their touch, their art if you will, of how to be a dynamic female and own their shit. In a world as tough as this, it's understandable how easy it can be to play into stereotypes, and allow others to dictate your thoughts and behavior. Understand that there is no shame in being who you want to be, but please do it with a certain level of confidence and panache! Know that at the end of the day, you were born with two X chromosomes, and that is a gift.

What other entity can bring forth life, sacrifice herself to care for others, and still find time to salvage one hell of a deal at their favorite department store? A fierce badass woman, that's who.

As each generation of women comes forth, I notice that mothers are not teaching their daughters the basics of what makes a well-rounded woman, and young girls are losing touch with what differentiates them from the opposite sex. Perhaps, those mothers were not taught themselves; understandably, as generation after generation has been subjugated and dumbed-down through the years, but at some point, each female needs to look at herself in the mirror and ask, "Who am I?", "What do I want?" and "How can I honor this life that was given to me?"

I understand (and fully believe in) the importance of the women's movement, and the need for equality. When my grandmother was young, pregnant women had to leave their jobs, only certain career options and positions were available for ladies, and birth control (along with information on it) was illegal in most states! It's difficult for me to fathom these impediments living now as a young woman, and when you look around at the state of things, how far have we as a gender truly come? Even today, March 8th

2017, as I sit here and go over the final draft of this book, it is "A Day without a Woman." A day when people all over are *still* fighting and marching for the rights of females.

When I asked my grandmother for her thoughts on this matter, she said, "back in my day, there was NO women's choice and a very real glass ceiling." It was, and still is, a goal to equalize the genders; one is no more important than the other. Though one could say the same thing for racial issues. In my mind, it's not so much a matter of equality in men versus women, as much as it's a matter of equality for all humanity, no matter their skin color or anatomy underneath their clothing. I feel the true question is *why* has it taken us so long to move ahead so very little? Why is the push back on equality for humanity so vicious and closed-minded? After all, no matter what your beliefs, don't we all come into this world the same way?

Without going too off topic and getting back to the women's movement, Gloria Steinem once said "Some of us are becoming the men we wanted to marry," and I think it's so true! Through the years, the original ideas of the feminist movement have become so lost in translation that many of us have fallen into the "men are stupid" school of thought, which makes us just as sexist as the opposite gender we are blaming. That's not what the movement was originally about. Initially, women's liberation was a campaign calling for reform on several issues that had plagued the female gender for centuries. Feminism called for equal rights and equal pay, reproductive rights, ending sexual harassment and violence against women, just to name a few items on the docket.

It's sad, however, that despite the brutal fight women of the movement put up, many of today's young female population know nothing of the suffrage movement or women's lib. Instead, they strive for things like attention and instant gratification as opposed to an education that could bring them so much farther. Know it deep in your bones what you yearn for, ladies! Have a dream and never stop educating yourself. Education is so important, no matter what your interest. An educated female is a powerful weapon that can wield strength and revolution. When they push you down and say you cannot do something, get back up and prove them wrong. Women achieve greatness every day; so why be the wallflower when you can be a tiger, eyes gleaming with success and fierceness? Think about it…

Unfortunately, in the strenuous push for equality and independence, women seem to have lost the appreciation for their gender. Just because a woman can cook and clean does not mean that she should be confined to the household for eternity, but it becomes unbalanced when she cannot cook at all and finds anything "girly" to be unfavorable. Why must the term "girly" get such a negative connotation these days, and how have we allowed shame to be associated with it? Men created this term and use it to deem something or someone as weak or lesser. Over the years, if something or someone is called "girly," females are the first to stand up in outrage, prompting the men to snicker and shake their heads even more. If you don't like the word, then don't use it, but I feel women should not be ashamed to be too feminine or too tough. Just be you.

No matter my mood, I do strive every day to be better and know myself, as every person should. I'm grateful to have a plethora of women in my life that are profoundly amazing, and deeply care for my well-being. I have many aunties, second mothers, sisters and girlfriends who have seen me through the darkest days as well as the lightest. These angels keep me real, keep me safe and most importantly, have taught me to love and respect other women. Real queens respect other queens. These strong women have helped me discover my own inner power and have stood by me as I learn the lessons that one must as she grows from maidenhood to adulthood. Now knowing all of their different opinions on what an awesome woman is, here is a little taste of my own…

ESSENCE OF A GODDESS

In this first section, we will discuss the inner workings of what makes an amazing woman, from health and beauty, to breakups and self-defense. I wanted to share the insights and opinions from both myself as well as those of other women. A female is at her most powerful when she begins with the roots that ground her. To cultivate a presence of greatness, she must commence from a place of honesty. It is only then that true beauty is birthed.

CHAPTER ONE

BODY BY... YOU!

It's been said time and time again that no matter your size or shape, you should love and worship your body - it is, after all, your temple. I know that we as women constantly hear this message, but most of us don't take it to heart and truly believe it. When I say *truly believe it*, I mean really taking the time, at least once a day, to appreciate the fact that your heart continues to beat, whether you ask it to or not. Your immune system works overtime to process not only the toxins from your environment, but also everything you put into your body from the pesticides and sugars in foods, to the lotions and sprays you use on yourself. Your muscles and bones take all the wear and tear from gym workouts, having sex, bearing children and the natural process of aging. Despite life's daily grind, we need to remind ourselves to be grateful for our bodies, and love them as they are.

Chapter One

If we want to change them, we can, but first, love your temple. I'm one of those women that will tell you, if you want to change your body, then go for it! I am not one to judge if a woman wants bigger or smaller breasts, or if she wants to get her knees lifted at 40- it's not my body. However, in saying that, if you chose to alter your body, be in your element and power when doing so. When you walk down the street, rock that body! Even at your local grocery store, walk down those aisles like you're on the damn catwalk if you need to. Your body is indeed a gift and far more valuable than anything money can buy. People will always have their opinions, but screw 'em. You get one body and when your due date is up, it's on to the next adventure. So, enjoy this one while you're on it.

Just so I don't get my ass sued, here's a quick DISCLAIMER: The information in this chapter is not intended as a substitute for the medical advice of physicians. The reader should regularly consult a physician in matters relating to his/her health and particularly, with respect to any symptoms that may require diagnosis or medical attention. The fitness information in this chapter is meant to supplement, not replace, proper fitness training. Like any sport involving speed and equipment, balance and environmental factors pose some inherent risk. The author advises readers to take full responsibility for their safety, and know their limits. Before practicing the workout techniques described in this chapter, be sure that you do not take risks beyond your level of experience, aptitude, training and comfort level.

WHO'S THAT CHICK?

It took me over 15 years to figure out how to have "a healthy body image," and I still continue to work on it every day. I grew up in the ballet world, where at the age of 11, I had to start counting calories and thinking about whether or not I should eat breakfast the following day.

Because of the pressure to be thin, my body dysmorphia evolved into pure craziness that I'm still not quite fully over. I've been through eating disorders, countless hours of therapy and yo-yoing through my clothing sizes. I have had people tell me my ass was too big or too small and so much more. When all is said and done, I had to find out for myself what type of body I wanted, and how to fight for it. Did I want to drop ten pounds? Well then, I had to work for it. Did I want to eat a pint of ice cream because I was sad? Well, I could, but I had to be aware of what it would do to my side ass in the morning. The list goes on and on, but the major point, first and foremost, was my mental attitude towards my physical self. The first step in working towards my ideal body was to let go of my fears. Fear of failing to be a size zero, fear

Chapter One

of relapsing on my current diet, and a fear of losing that perfect body once I had it.

In my early twenties, I went through a very tough breakup in Brooklyn and ended up moving to Florida, Miami to be exact. I lived with a close girlfriend of mine, and I was a complete hot mess. Wine and cigarettes were my breakfast followed by a heavy dose of starving myself, then overeating. After the initial shock over what had occurred, I randomly decided to start running outside every day. At first, the ritual was more of an escape from reality where I would just run, listen to Tori Amos, and, of course, cry a whole bunch. After a while though, the tears subsided and running became a happier thing for me. I looked forward to it; it helped my mental state and got me away from everyone for a bit.

During my run one day, I had the simple realization that I was getting in my own way. It came to me so easily and I felt an immediate release. I saw how my body was changing for the better, even though I wasn't focused on eating healthy, counting calories or even weighing myself. My clothes fit in a more desirable manner and my spirits were looking up again. I imagined how little baby Alex would react if I treated her the way I had been treating my current self. I thought about the words that had been coming out of my mouth, such as "I will *never* lose enough weight to fit into those jeans," and found out that I was not only getting in my own way, but I also didn't *want* to let go of the fear of failing. I then became aware that the struggle for me wasn't just about being fat or skinny; it was the pure state of my mental attitude that had been holding me back. I was neither fat nor skinny, just lost somewhere in between in an unhappy purgatory of shit. What it really all came down to was what shape and size felt good for me. I had to *feel* that calmness of certainty, knowing that I would eventually create the body I wanted to live in.

Media never helps to make it easier on women either; always pushing us to be skinnier or curvier. Whether through magazines, online articles, ad campaigns or film and television; the pressure to fit a mold is in our faces on the daily. The trouble lies in the fact that in this technology driven era, there's no stopping the media train.

I'm of the belief that no matter your size, you should own it and find joy in knowing your body is yours. Barring any medical conditions, you alone can change your body whenever you want, you just have to *want to*. The media will be what it will be. The challenge is in rising above feeling pressured to be any other size than what feels comfortable to you. In the past several years, there has been a slight shift in the direction towards welcoming any and all body types; though it may not have made a huge dent yet, it is a beginning. A beginning to end of a most serious struggle that has affected the female gender for what seems like forever; disgust and dysmorphia with one's self-image.

Through countless years of struggling with my self-image and weight, I eventually figured out that my body responds best to hard-core cardio (aka running, dancing, kickboxing etc.) and lots of stretching. I've also always enjoyed dancing, and it doesn't matter to me if it's in the club, at a house party or in front of my own mirror. To this day, dancing is my number one "go-to" workout. So, find out what makes your body respond and stick to it! While not everyone's body is the same, I've picked out two great exercises that you can do almost anywhere: planes, hotel rooms, the subway (my sister says this is a lawsuit waiting to happen), your apartment or the gym, to tone and firm.

Arms: Put your arms behind you, with palms facing up. Make sure your core is engaged and your shoulders are down. In this position, you have the option to pulse upward, inward, or to make small circles and crosses with both arms. The length of this exercise depends on your current fitness level. <u>For beginners</u>, start out with thirty second intervals. Do three reps and make sure to stretch out your triceps in between and after. <u>For advanced</u>, start with one-minute intervals until the burn is too much (usually around three or four reps). Make sure to stretch after!

Legs & Stomach: Planks! You all know what it is and it works. Planks are a simple and meditative exercise to strengthen your body, especially your core. Hold this position for as long as you can. When you get more advanced, you can do side planks or planks on one foot. Planks are a good way to warm up your body temperature without having to run a bunch of miles.

Have you limbered up lately? Stretch and make sure to keep limber throughout life. It's much easier to injure yourself on a simple hike or gym visit if you don't regularly stretch. People usually peg me for a dancer right away, either from my posture, or by the fact that I am constantly stretching. Stretching your muscles after a hot shower or bath is a perfect time; take five minutes to touch your toes, stretch your calves and quadriceps.

See those fun photos below! It is also advisable to keep your back and hips pliable to avoid sexual injuries. They happen more often than you think!

Chapter One

What I've learned from my own experiences, lord knows I've had enough of them, is not to ignore the cause of health problems and treat only the symptoms. As a crazy Gemini woman constantly on the go, I've had mono, multiple torn hamstrings, severe knee injuries, bronchial infections, a broken tailbone and so much more. With only attempting to treat my symptoms, I was usually sick or injured longer than was necessary. I highly recommend finding out (to the best of your ability) what the actual root of your ailment is. As much as the dancer in me loves them, it doesn't always help to just pop a painkiller. When you are hurt or sick, the mainstream way nowadays to fix it is to just take some medication without necessarily discovering what the true issue is. Granted if you break your ankle; it's broken, no question there. But if you are susceptible to getting headaches every day, look into why that might be instead of shoveling over the counter candy in your mouth every couple of hours. Go to your doctor, try alternative medicine or holistic sources (acupuncture is my favorite modality) and look to things like your diet, sleeping habits and stress levels. More often than not, stress is a *huge* culprit. Stress produces cortisol, which is like poison in the body. It flows through your blood stream in unbalanced levels when you get stressed and is very detrimental to both your mental and physical state. FYI: stress is also a huge culprit in the aging process, which leads me to…

MIRROR, MIRROR ON THE WALL

A couple years back, I had a startling discovery one day while plucking my eyebrows. I was looking at my face in the mirror and seeing lines in places that used to be as smooth as a baby's bottom! Now, I realize that a baby's bottom could have wrinkles, but those are cute wrinkles that will disappear. These lines seemed permanent and no amount of makeup was covering them. "Noooooooooooooo," I screamed in horror, realizing that these noticeable differences on my face were none other than the beginning stages of the aging process. I couldn't believe it when it happened, was I at that age already? I didn't know quite how to face the reality of what was occurring - literally.

Since this day, all sorts of alterations have appeared on my chest, neck and face. I feel like I should insert a million of those horror face emojis here. With such sensitive and fair skin, it's been somewhat of an uphill battle. I can't just douse myself in a variety of oils, or poke and prod my face and décolletage with age-defying tools, my skin will freak out. Instead, I make sure to keep out of the sun as much as possible, and consciously work on not wrinkling my forehead when I speak (not an easy thing for an actor).

As women, we tend to joke about aging, but I know for most of us, it's never a fun topic when it comes to the physical aspect. Many of my older female friends and

Chapter One

family have been instrumental in steering me the right way to the fountain of youth. My friends who are beauty bloggers always tell me to use Vitamin C on my face, whether it's in liquid or mask form. Along with that, *pure hyaluronic acid serum* has helped to slow the appearance of aging a bit, as it plumps and hydrates skin. "Restoration is key as we age," my mom says. My mother also taught me to steam my face when I was younger, which I love doing if I have the time. Make sure to do it carefully, but definitely steam those faces as often as possible. You can do it in the steam room, over a cup of hot liquid with a towel over your head, or with a professional at a spa.

I will readily admit that watching my face age has given me an uncertain fear. I know it's part of life, but it's not fun. I like things that are fun! All the women I know with beautiful skin have shared their secrets with me, which often include keeping healthy diets and managing the shit out of their skin. Nothing less. They use seaweed, placentas, fillers, herbs, lasers, you name it - aging gracefully is a full-time job, people.

NEMESES

On the topic of healthy diets, my body does not respond well at all to dairy or sugar. I know many women who respond similarly, so I don't feel so alone. I'm not lactose intolerant or a diabetic (thank goodness), but when I ingest these ingredients, my nose gets super stuffy and my face breaks out. Letting go of dairy has been easy for me, unless I'm craving nachos, however, my addiction to sugar has been another demon all together. Sugar is my drug of choice but, like most drugs, my body can't handle too much of it. I try not indulging too often, but gummies and caramel just make my life so much sweeter, literally.

To help stave off all the reactions I face if and when I give in to my addiction, I take lots of vitamins and drink a shit ton of water to assist my liver in processing the attack I just thrust upon it. In any case, sugar or not, I do recommend to women that you nourish your body well, and take all appropriate dietary supplements that are right for you. Vitamins B, C, D, E are essentials to assist and support the immune response, healthy muscle metabolism and tissue regeneration within the human body. To keep the relationship between sugar and myself in check, I often will go for a week or two and try to keep sugar out of my diet. Instead, I consume lots of fresh foods and indulge in some personal favorites that are expensive like sushi and kale chips. When I'm having a massive withdrawal (usually by day three of no sugar intake), I'll treat myself to a fancy coffee or have some healthy potato chips; the salt often helps to stave off thinking about my long lost love- SUGAR.

Chapter One

While the babies of the 80's were fed diets of commercial formula and *Gerber* baby food, my parents were ahead of the curve, feeding little baby Alex spirulina mixed into foods like applesauce and yogurt. Spirulina is a blue-green micro-alga filled with lots of protein, minerals and vitamins that has been steadily making its way into popularity with health-conscious crowds. It can be taken in tablet, powder or flake form and makes a great addition to smoothies, juices and snacks. Besides keeping the tablets with me, in case my blood sugar decides to crash, or mixing it up with some apple juice to drink on the go, I really enjoy using spirulina in my face masks. My favorite face mask is mixing spirulina with some zinc and a little bit of water. Zinc is good for reducing inflammation and repairing cells. You can get zinc at any vitamin shop, health food store or online. I'll usually take half a capsule of zinc powder, add a tablespoon of spirulina, and a couple drops of water at a time and mix until it's a smooth consistency. Don't add too much water but make sure there is enough to make the mixture pasty. Apply this mixture to your face (not by your eyes!) and let dry for 5-10 minutes or so. When you feel it start to crack when you smile, gently rinse off with warm water and voila! Fresh faced skin!

Note: It can get messy when you wash it off and is sometimes easier to rinse off in the shower. As healthy as spirulina is, I would highly recommend drinking lots of water when you take it. Without enough water, it can constipate and dehydrate you very quickly.

YOUR BREAST FRIENDS

Whether large, small or in-between, our breasts are very important and we should treat them as we would a best friend - if not better! Breasts are beautiful and much too often, taken for granted. Even we women don't always appreciate them. In an age where breast cancer is a rapidly growing disease, it's crucial that we take the health of our breasts into our own hands, literally.

- Massage your breasts daily, or have your partner do it- what fun! Castor oil, dandelion oil and even some salves containing medicinal cannabis are some of my favorites among many wonderful options. If you can massage them at least twice a week, your breasts will be happier and the tissue will be relieved of harmful toxins. Plus, who doesn't love a great breast massage now and again?

- Drinking plenty of water and exercising daily are two things that assist in getting rid of toxins within the system. No matter how filtered your city's water is, tap water can contain chlorine, metals, hormones and other chemicals. I keep a water filter on my showerhead at home and make sure to try and drink only filtered water whether home or out and about.

- When and if you can, wear bras with no underwire. The underwire constricts your lymphatic fluids; and if the wire is actual metal, the long-term harmful consequences can be exacerbated. Due to these scary facts, I started buying comfy wireless bras from *Victoria's Secret* a couple of years back.

- Do your research and find the appropriate supplements you can take to support healthy breast tissue and control inflammation. Antioxidants like garlic, green tea and dark leafy vegetables like spinach, kale and broccoli have been recommended to me by several health specialists and doctors.

- Calcium D Gluconate helps to detoxify the body. It is a great anti-cancer supplement.

- Omega-3 Fatty Acids: You can find in these fatty acids in foods like flax seeds, walnuts and fish such as, wild salmon, sardines and tuna. You can also go to a vitamin shop or a health food store and purchase some fish oil capsules to take. Make sure that the manufacturer tests their fish oil so that it doesn't contain toxic heavy metals like mercury and cadmium. *Renew Life* and *Nature's Way* are two great companies I like to purchase from.

- For any busy lady, it can be hard to keep focused on what she is putting into her body, chemical wise, but even the smallest changes make a difference. Harmful chemicals do not make for happy breasts!

- Pay attention to things like your laundry detergent- does it have perfumes and dyes? Your deodorant- is it filled with aluminum?

You and you alone must take responsibility for your own breast health, so make sure to also do your monthly breast exams!

RULE OF THUMB

Whether it's through your skin, weight, sleeping habits, bodily functions or even attitude, whatever you put into your body you will get back. If you treat your body with vitamins, healthy food options and lots of sleep, it will be noticeable. However, if you consume a diet of crap, don't sleep enough and continuously party with cigarettes and booze, those around you will smell, see, and be made aware of your naughty ways. Not everything that comes out of your body though, is necessarily bad. For example, if you know you have a big date or an event coming up where you might be sweating or breathing on people, don't consume a lot of garlic the previous days before. Garlic odors can make an appearance once you start sweating and trust me, people can smell it.

Our goal should always be to love ourselves and keep a healthy lifestyle. This will assist in feeling better overall and hopefully, living a longer life. When you have clean insides, and keep your body in motion, it will never grow old, no matter what age you find yourself at. When you can, walk or bike instead of driving, take the stairs instead of the escalator, and be creative with your calories if you are watching what you eat. And no matter what age you reach, keep dancing! Dancing is wonderful for your physical and mental states, your energy levels and your overall fun-loving self. Last, but certainly not least, age is just a number. What matters is how we feel inside and how well we treat our temples. The body is an amazing universe unto itself. With physical and mental effort, respect and love, you can become a magnificent embodiment of beauty and power, both inside and out.

CHAPTER TWO

MISS MANNERS

I don't care if you're an heiress on the upper east side of Manhattan or work at the local hockey rink in Houlton, Maine (yes, I know people there), there is a time and place in each and every woman's life where a level of sophistication should exist- no exceptions. You don't need to be a *Mensa* level genius to know things like your napkin should be placed on your lap, that it's rude to interrupt a person while talking, or that you should not be on your phone during a meal with company. There are several etiquette rules, however, that I see people trespass on daily. This book is basically about women, and in this chapter, we'll discuss certain manners that a lady should always keep in her back pocket. You won't need to utilize them at all times, but a female should be aware of what her present location and circumstance require.

Chapter Two

Historically, there was a more pressing reason for the manners and etiquette that we now know of, and utilize today. Birthed largely from the royal courts in Europe, if there was a unified way of *how* to do something, there was order and a set of standards that people had to abide by. Manners, as we know them today, were created by the upper class out of necessity. In highly populated cities especially, violence and crude behaviors were common and the aristocrats needed a way to distinguish themselves from the lower classes.

It was one of their ways to control the craziness. If everyone was polite and followed orders, as according to their station, peace and comfort for the affluent would be more readily available. Chances are, you're not visiting King Charles II in his palace tomorrow, so not to worry, but there is still no excuse for ladies without manners! Having manners is essentially having awareness and a level of respect for those around you. In this chapter, we will discuss several do's and don'ts that make a great lady really stand apart from her peers.

I'm pretty sure this is the longest chapter in the book because there are so many obvious basics that ladies constantly ignore. You don't necessarily have to know which fork is for the salad and which is for the dessert, but it helps to be aware of the basics that really bring out your sophisticated side.

POSTURE

You don't have to attend etiquette classes to know that slouching is wrong. It's not only horrible for you anatomically, but it also doesn't look good. Slouching can bring about headaches and will give the impression to those around you that you don't care and are not present. One of the reasons why people's guts start to grow larger as they age is because they get lazy and don't sit up straight. Just FYI. Throughout your day, wherever you are sitting or even standing for that matter, try to think of a string at the top of your head being pulled upwards towards the ceiling. It will assist in lengthening your torso, without shoving your spine erect and hurting yourself. Women should stand up straight, not because it's what's expected from us, but because it gives us a presence. The way you hold your body has an effect on your mood and the energy you give off. Your brain is altered depending on how your body is positioned, so stand tall and stand proud. A lady who stands up straight is more powerful to the populous than a hunchback who doesn't give a damn.

Chapter Two

HEADS UP!

Part of standing up straight is keeping your head (which is a mighty heavy part of the human body) upright and not always looking down at your phone. One of my first jobs when I was a teenager was at a market research office. We had all sorts of crazy characters around the office, mainly women. I was at a young impressionable age, and many of those women taught me valuable lessons, mainly on what *not* to do with my life. There was one lady who came to work with us for a short period of time, let's call her Nicole. Nicole was a tough Italian broad who had previously worked at the state penitentiary, and she was a riot. This beautiful soul taught me something very important that stuck with me till this very day. I was walking down the hallway, completely oblivious to the fact that I was looking at the ground when I heard a voice behind me saying, "Pick your head up, girl. Why you walkin' with your head down?" "What?" I said, "My head's not down." Nicole said, "Yeah it is. You should always walk with your head up and look proud. Command your space or others will take advantage of you." She went on to tell me that if you walk with your head down in prison, you could get jumped because people see weakness. She told me to always hold my head up, be aware and know that I was not one to be messed with. Since then, I make it a point to walk with my head up, and am attentive to the goings on around me. I learned this when I was 14, so it's never too early or late to start!

HOLD UP

They say patience is a virtue, but I think she's a tough mistress who's difficult to master. Needless to say, patience has never been my strong point, but it's such an asset to have in your arsenal of qualities as a lady. Over the years, I have forced myself to get better at it. Whether it's dealing with incompetence, learning a new skill or facing issues with your significant other, having the patience to get through it calmly, instead of yelling, cussing and looking like a fool makes a world of difference. While patience is a very admirable quality, use it within reason of course. There are times when a lady must put her foot down and tell idiots what's what.

A CONVERSATIONAL PIECE

Women have a lot to say. Unfortunately, we don't always get our point across the way we had intended. Women should be able to say what they mean, but many of us are always so busy trying to please everyone, a behavior society ingrained into our gender from birth. If we are too forceful, or sure of ourselves in our delivery, we are automatically labeled *the bitch*. I've been there one too many times. However, if we are timid, then we become *the likeable pushovers.* How can we win? In achieving a healthy balance, I like to make sure I maintain my position while not making the conversation awkward, if possible. Anyone who knows me knows I DESPISE awkward situations with a deep dark passion. If something has gone awry, I feel a lady should make an effort to discover the miscommunication.

While we are on the topic of conversation, for some reason, many women don't know when to shut the f*ck up! YEEESSSSS, we should all be able to speak our mind, but too often, I'll see women bogarting the conversation and making it a monologue. Have you ever sat in a public venue, and actually listened in on a conversation between women? There doesn't seem to be much of an exchange going on, hence the word, *monologue*. While I'm sure people could judge some of my conversations, I genuinely care and want to know other's thoughts and experiences. It's all about substance.

Male or female, trust me, no one wants to listen to the 45-minute story about your "slutcation" down by the shore when you were eighteen. As Mr. Bennet in Pride and Prejudice stated to his emo daughter Mary, "That will do extremely well, child. You have delighted us long enough. Let the other young ladies have time to exhibit." After all, having the courtesy to listen to others while they ramble on is sometimes handy. You never know when that person might have a little gem of wisdom to unknowingly share. Also, those that listen don't tend to talk as much, you can learn a ton that way. When you are in a group of people, always look for the one who has said the least. They are usually gathering information and paying attention to what everyone has said around them.

P.S. To all the men reading this book, when you are trying to woo a girl, she never wants to hear about your past sexual experiences, no matter how cool she is. It's not the gentlemanly thing to do. If you're trying to get into her pants, don't tell her about another girl's pants… or lack thereof. It's not amusing to us, nor does it make us want to be another notch on the old bedpost. You sir, are probably not James Bond and if you were, you wouldn't talk about your past conquests to possible future bed partners. Be smooth and make her feel like she's the only one that matters.

LEFT WING, RIGHT WING OR SOMEWHERE IN BETWEEN

When starting a conversation with a singular person or group of people she doesn't know well, I feel a lady should keep her political and religious beliefs to herself.

Chapter Two

Unless you know for an absolute fact, beyond all doubt, that the group of people you are sitting with are of a like mind, DO NOT talk politics or religion while out and about. These two topics will get you in a world of trouble no matter which side of the table you are on. I know so many women, and many of my friends, will disagree on this, but I still stand by the idea that politics and religion are dangerous conversation starters - especially these days! Those two topics are so volatile that they have been known to end friendships and business deals. Unless you are aiming to be the secretary-general of the United Nations or the next president of our country, don't tread in those waters, till you know who you're swimming with. When was the last time you had a chat with someone who brought up abortions and immigrants, or immigrants having abortions while smoking marijuana, that ended well? On the flip side, if you know that the person or party you are conversing with is open-minded and receptive, regardless of their beliefs or views, then those discussions are acceptable. The goal should not be to sway them to your side or to prove that you are right and they are wrong. The aim of your educated exchange should always be to learn and grow, and if a conversation containing these topics can facilitate that, then, by all means, dive right in.

MIND YOUR OWN BEESWAX, RAMONA

A lady prying into another's business makes her quite rude and annoying. If someone wants to share something with you, they will. If you feel they want to share, but are holding back, there is no harm in questioning politely, but don't be all up in every person's business. It is so uncomfortable to be on the receiving end of someone trying to check out what's happening on your phone screen, or even worse, listening to your conversations. My girlfriends and I used to go to this cute breakfast place all the time, until we started to notice one of waitresses would always hang around and listen to us talk. She thought she was being sly and that we hadn't noticed, but we certainly did. Needless to say, we don't frequent that place anymore. If you really, *really* must know something, a sophisticated lady will get her information either by crafty wits or really good sleuthing. Take your pick.

THEY'VE EARNED IT

I don't care what anyone says, a real woman respects her elders. Though it may not seem like it, there is always wisdom somewhere in something of what our elders share with us. Women should learn the traditions, lessons and trials of life from all the women that came before them. Though, not all their anecdotes may float your boat, there can sometimes be jewels of wisdom if you listen carefully. Previous generations have often been through more struggles than us, and I feel it's immensely important to show them the respect their age and experience has garnered.

SEND MY COMPLIMENTS TO THE HOST

A nice gesture that I think compliments a stunning personality is being gracious. You can be a hospitable host, kind to others, volunteer and (most importantly in my book) you can also write thank-you notes. A handwritten thank-you note goes a long way. With all of the technology we have nowadays, you rarely see a handwritten anything anymore. I know people who don't know how to write in cursive, or can barely use any writing tools because everything can be done from their phone, computer or tablet. To take the time to write a small note in your own hand is a beautiful gesture. It's personal and shows that you truly appreciate the other person's actions.

If you're going to someone's house for a meal or party, a gracious act is to make sure to bring a little something. Whether it be flowers, a bottle of wine, or an edible treat, never show up empty-handed if you have been invited.

F*CKING SH*T

Like many people out there, I don't like being told I can't do something. Swearing for women is generally thought of as vulgar and a definite no-no. But I say fucking go for it IF the circumstances and present company are appropriate for that. When I teach dance classes to children, you won't hear any cursing out of my mouth till my car door is shut and I'm headed home. If I am chatting it up with my bestie, or even a family member, chances are the Bostonian in me will come out, accompanied by many colorful curse words. I try to be courteous when hanging out with certain friends who may not be comfortable with certain words. One word in particular that many people here in America are offended by is the word "cunt." I want to talk about this for a moment because the actual word means "a woman's genitals." Hello ladies! Wake up! This term is not dirty or horrible. It's just a word like "bitch" that if used in a certain context, may seem vulgar, but is actually describing something normal in this world. So please, know that being offended by the word *cunt* just gives it power in a negative way. This is just as demeaning. I understand that it's not the body part so much as the *way* the term is being used, but then, don't use it and make sure to buy a pair of earmuffs before going abroad because they use that word all the time.

All in all, you don't have to live like an absolute debutante, nor must you resign yourself to a life of perfectionism. However, with that being said, women who take the time to write a thank-you note or don't mind listening once in a while instead of always doing the talking are often appreciated more for their manners and consideration. No matter your background, all women have the ability to present themselves with poise, power and graciousness. So, get out there and *wow* the shit out of them!

CHAPTER THREE

LOYALTY

It doesn't matter the age, ethnicity, background or disposition, when it comes down to it, about 70% of women I know (or have met in passing) are not loyal to other women. That is some bullshit, hence, why I wrote this chapter. On any given day, when you turn on the news, you will see that when certain ethnic groups are persecuted, they stand firm as one. Even men will stand together when loyalty is needed, regardless of the cause. It doesn't even matter if the guys had beef with each other in the past, when push comes to shove, they are there for one another. Women don't quite seem to comprehend that concept of unity. Instead, we tend to find comfort in putting the group at odds with one another, and pushing our sisters down instead of helping them rise. We judge our own kind as if it was bred into our nature. Who's prettier? Who can be the most popular? The competition really heats up when you throw men, money and children into the mix.

I'm not saying that I didn't do stupid things to other girls when I was younger, but I've learned as I age that when the shit hits the fan, you want your girls to be there for you. You truly discover who your real friends are when your life takes a tough turn. When you go through a severe break up, lose your job suddenly, or a friend betrays you, this is when women should stand by each other and yet, so often, they don't.

When it comes to being my friend, if you can't handle the heat, get the hell out of the kitchen. I would go to great lengths to take care of my girlfriends, not only because I consider many of them my family, but I also found out that when women support each other, great things can happen. I'm all too familiar, as are most of us, with difficult situations like breakups, deaths and career struggles. Too often though, I have counted on "friends" that turned out to be unreliable. Knowing how awful that feels, I would never want to impart that to another woman who considered me supportive and trustworthy.

Many women are not strong enough to stand up for one another, simply because they are cowards. They would rather hide or take the easy road out of a situation than stand up beside their sisters, and deal with the issue at hand. This weakness, or possible lack of awareness, is really a plague upon female evolution. The fact that we don't stand together and instead, allow the pettiest shit to come between us is sick. It's not a complicated thing! You do not have to devote your entire existence to another being, it's simply knowing where your allegiance lies and what you will do to keep that bond of trust between you and a sister friend.

Women, especially young women these days, tend to "cheat" on one another, if you will. Girls can be completely ruthless, often worse than boys.

Even though women have been stabbing each other in the back for centuries, cruelties like female bullying, slut shaming and social alienation are on the rise now more than ever. It hits me right in the gut when I see young people who have been so shamed and bullied by their peers that they turn to suicide or other harmful options. Where is the kindness and compassion? Despite this vile reality, there is also a growing awareness within society aiming to bring sisterhood, equality and respect for females to the masses. How can we expect respect from the male population if we cannot give that to one another first?

Competition between females is almost a given from a young age, and being a *successful* woman doesn't make things any easier in adulthood. The media, the business world and so on pit women against each other and the unfortunate fact remains that a woman usually feels she must take down any other women near or in her way, on the road to the top. Thankfully, there have only been two events in my life where backstabbing women left their mark, but twice was more than enough. Both times, I found it sad but fascinating to look into the eyes of the traitor I once considered a good friend. To see her pupils dilate with fear when confronted. She knew what she did was beyond wrong. I'm amazed at how instead of facing her wrongdoing and owning up to it so that the wound may be mended, she cowered and turned away as though she was shopping for produce at the market. It's mind-blowing, really.

Why can't women be happy for one another's achievements? What are they so afraid of? Jealously is a slimy bug that will catch up with the weak-minded sooner or later. While I will admit that it's not always easy to see others readily get what you've been busting your ass to achieve, jealousy is an ugly accessory that no woman needs. The irony is that, if women did stand with one another, we could progress so much farther in this world. You can see great examples of this in strong friendships between women because the loyalty is there. Female unity is more than just not hating on other women; it's about respecting and trusting one another. Unity can be found when we support each other through both our darkest and lightest days. Sometimes, support is really just allowing our sisters to be themselves, and accepting their beauty and their demons, both inside and out.

That said, there will always be shady bull-shitters. Though competition can definitely be healthy, be a woman who raises other women up, instead of throwing them under the bus to get ahead. Now, that's progress. Helping other's flames to grow does not diminish your own! If we can all remember that and put it into practice, then imagine what could be accomplished for women all over the world.

My sister wrote a poem that I feel captures the essence of what this chapter is about. It does not need a major introduction, as the artistic soul encompassing it is transparent.

BOTH HANDS OVER MY EYES

the truth
the fucking truth

to encourage against one's best interests,
to believe against all odds,
to know when it is time to move on.

how saintly we may be,
in our subservience. how
truthful we may be, in our loyalty.
how to know the difference…

poison shows its true colors
marginal love makes no waves.
forgive and
forget and
forgive again,

but know what awaits you
in the depth of dreams.
know what you have done,
know what you have lost,
know your capabilities.
know the truth.

CHAPTER FOUR

CAN YOU RELATE?

When you look up the word *courtship* in the dictionary, it's typically defined as "A period during which a couple develop a romantic relationship, especially with a view to marriage." Or "Behavior designed to persuade someone to marry or develop a romantic relationship with one." Though you might view this as old fashioned, there is something to be said for the historical ways of courting. Not that men are the only ones who can pursue, nor must they do all the work, but let's face it, today's younger generations of men basically have it handed to them by us. Yes, we females readily give men attention, sex and devotion; the whole kit and caboodle before they even know what we do for a living. Therefore, they have lost their need to do any work when it comes to us women. Why would you work hard for a million dollars if it were handed to you on the regular, wrapped in a bow? If you look out in nature for example, it's the male peacocks that must flaunt their beauty to prove their worth to the females. Not the other way around. In the past few generations, women have downgraded their self-worth, and made it so easy for men. Like a puppy trying to please, we work overtime to accommodate them and make things easy. It's fine for a man to be shy, those guys usually need a bit of encouragement and kindness. It's also awesome if a girl is confident and forward with her feelings; make the first move! We are more than capable. The problem is, if a guy is always waiting for the ladies to come to him, then that's just flat out fucking lazy, and if he's lazy in the beginning, it will probably only get worse in the future.

On the flip side of this thought, no matter where you are in the world, you'll always be able to find a woman who will tell you she wants to be *respected*. By "respected," many females mean they want their doors opened, they want accolades and flowers with petals of perfection. Some women, however, want more than just tangible objects. They want their significant other to worship, love and adore them, whether they have proven themselves worthy of that treatment or not. These women expect their men to be their slaves as opposed to their equals. They want their man crawling over broken glass to bring them lemonade. It's a bit too much in my book, but that's just how some women like it. Though the broken glass fantasy may be a bit eccentric for some, there is merit in the idea of allowing (and expecting) your partner to go the extra mile to make sure you know they are dedicated. It's a fabulous feeling to know that your partner is willing to work for your love, body, and attention; whatever it may be that you want. Now, while it's true that all human beings should respect one another, I must ask you this, are you deserving of the attention and devotion you are asking for? While this may sound harsh to some, get over it and honestly ask yourself, have you *earned* that respect? Do you treat yourself that way? Do you treat your partner the way they would like to be treated? Love can't just be a one-way street… at least not in my book. Literally.

CONFUSION & COMMUNICATION

I cannot count the amount of times I've heard a guy start his sentence with, "Don't be offended when I say this, but," followed by a compliment on my physical appearance or personality. I was confused for so long as to why guys felt it necessary to start with a comment of apology. I eventually realized it was because, more often than not, they themselves were subconsciously (or consciously) confused and concerned. Some men don't want to dish out a compliment and then in turn, offend us or come off as a sex-driven dog. Men are not mind readers, and what is acceptable and appropriate for each woman is personal. To be fair, there is a right and wrong way to compliment a lady, but after generations of sexual subjugation of the female gender, social norms are now blurred. What is okay for one female may not necessarily jive with another; some women expect their doors to be opened while others are so independent that they don't want a man near their door handles. I bring all this up because I feel it's important to clarify with the opposite sex how you expect to be treated. Then they will know how you roll… in and out of the bedroom.

As a Gemini, I believe that communication is key, without it, I get quite frustrated. I feel off when lines are crossed and information is inferred. While texting makes communication more accessible these days, I feel it also makes it more difficult in the sense that, you can never quite *know* the other person's real meaning behind their message. If I'm driving and want to be safe, I might just respond to my bestie with "k, girl," instead of "That suuuucks, girl. I'm so glad though, that you thought to cyber stalk the shit out of him, and found out he IS *unfortunately* married. Great looking out! I love you. Oh, and he's a piece of shit btw." Since I only wrote, "k, girl," my bestie could be thinking that I'm depressed, that I got pulled over, that I'm angry at her for uncovering this, or that I simply just don't care. Even though she knows me better than most, how would she know my true meaning through a text? Now, put that idea into a dating/new relationship scenario. It's stupid to just infer what you think you know about a person you met two weeks ago. Women LOVE to infer things through text; I do it ALL the time. I am so guilty of thinking I know what guys mean or what they are thinking when they text me, and I despise myself for it.

With every year that passes, I continue to work on my communication skills, especially when it comes to men. In the past, I had a habit of being compliant and avoiding conflict with the guy I was involved with. This stemmed from being a very fiery teenager who found nothing but drama and pain with every confrontation she brought to herself. In the years following, I wanted a drama-free life and made it a habit to avoid awkward conflicts with my signifi-cunt others (in this instance, yes, it's an insult). Moving forward, I strongly urge myself, and others, to face the fear of these uncomfortable situations. Be brave, honest and clear about what you are trying to communicate. This does not mean the outcome will always be in your favor, but at least, you spoke your truth, which, in hindsight, is a reward in itself.

KNOW YOUR SIGNS

Have you ever wondered why it's easier for you to get along with certain people more than others? Why some beings are so emotional and sensitive, while others are very stubborn and forceful. And why some of your relationships just haven't worked out, no matter how perfect everyone thought you were together. If so, a lot of it can be due to the combination of your astrological signs. Whether you believe in the spiritual side of life or not, astrology is much less of a metaphysical thing, and more of a multilayered scientific art. It's guided by the planets and stars, and has been utilized through the centuries in helping to correctly match couples. Today, this practice is still considered an important tool. For instance, many marriages in India are decided by the mother, father and a professional matchmaker. Astrological compatibility is a big part of the determining factor as to how well suited the couple might or might not be suited to each other.

My mom's best friend, whom my sister and I call Auntie Regina, is an amazing woman who has been through the fires of hell and back, and is still around to be a badass and share her wonderful energy with the world. She is an astrologer and none of the women in our family make any dating moves without first consulting her. You must know your signs! For example, I am not well suited to be romantically involved with any man whose sign is Taurus or Virgo because I am an air sign and he is earth. Want to understand how this works? There are many books and websites out there that you can search through to find out more information, but in this chapter, Auntie Regina compiled some short summaries for each sign to give you a glimpse into how astrology could affect your personal *and* professional life.

Astrology is not just for romantic relationships; it can also be useful for family, work or friend connections. There are several basic laws of Astrology that can help you to understand this science and use it to your benefit. To examine the process and get a general understanding of how well two people might get along, we will look at western astrology.

When considering the compatibility of two people, it is best to begin with both birth charts to get an idea of who they are as individuals and how they move through life. A *birth chart* is a grid-like diagram, or map, that shows where all the planets were during the time you were born. Having this information helps the astrologer see, for instance, if one or both people have big anger issues. If the astrologer noted this similarity, then this would be a match made in hell. Another typical method is to look at their *synastry chart*. The synastry chart is a grid that places each person's planets in proximity to that of the other's, helping the astrologer to better understand the dynamics at hand. This is an informative core tools used in evaluating compatibility. For the sake of generalizing and having a more simplistic approach to assessing your compatibility with another, let's just look at the basics…

First, both people will need to know their birth time, year and place of birth. *Astro.com* is a free source that caters to thousands of astrologers. From beginners to professionals, the site has an extremely active forum where you can learn as much or as little as you desire. You can put in your information, and it will pop off your birth chart. It also has a drop-down menu where you can choose the synastry chart.

You might then want to go to *cafeastrology.com* to read about what your "planet aspects," or combinations, mean. The four aspects are:

The Trine - A triangle like shape. This means a positive flow, an easy connection.

The Square - A square shape. This means challenging connections.

The Sextile - A star shape. This means exciting, positive connections.

Opposition - Two circles with a line connecting them, meaning opposites attract, this can be positive and/or challenging.

There are many astrology sites that will try to sell you a chart reading, and will attempt to lure you in with giving you a free small sample reading in hopes that you will desire to know more. Often, they will give you your planet line up once you input all the required birth information. You can do this for your love interest as well. Once you know both his and your sun, moon, Venus and Mars signs, you are ready to go to the next step to get a basic astrological assessment of whether you are a match made in heaven or hell.

One of the basic underlying principles in compatibility, that is quick and easy, is to look at the four elements associated with the zodiac signs. The elements are fire, air, water and earth. Part of understanding astrology is knowing that each astrological sign is both associated with a particular planet and one of the four elements. Here is the list of Astrological signs and their associated (ruling) planets and elements. From the first sign of the zodiac, in their respective order, we start with Aries. Please remember the dates are slightly different each year depending on the sun.

Sign	Date Range	Element	Ruled By
Aries	March 21-April 19	Fire	Mars
Taurus	April 20-May 20	Earth	Mercury
Gemini	May 21-June 20	Air	Mercury
Cancer	June 21-July 22	Water	The Moon
Leo	July 23-August 22	Fire	The Sun

Virgo	August 23-September 22	Earth	Mercury
Libra	September 23-October 22	Air	Venus
Scorpio	October 23-November 21	Water	Pluto
Sagittarius	November 22-December 21	Fire	Jupiter
Capricorn	December 22-January 19	Earth	Saturn
Aquarius	January 20-February 18	Air	Uranus
Pisces	February 19-March 20	Water	Neptune

Water signs are compatible with other water and earth signs. Water governs feelings, instincts, coolness, sensitivity and an attraction to understanding the nature of people and life, often realized through deeply felt observations. The water element is ruled through emotional sensitivity and a feeling of nature.

Air signs are compatible with other air signs and fire signs. Air governs thought, reasoning, logic, and attraction to academia. The Air element is emotionally ruled through a thinking process.

Earth signs are compatible with other earth and water signs. Earth governs the solid, sensuous, and unchanging. They like order, and have an attraction to that which is steadfast. The earth element is emotionally ruled by sensitivity to the ever-changing aspects of humanity and life.

Fire signs are compatible with other fire signs and air signs. Fire governs energy, creativity, spontaneity as well as boldness, heat and attraction to movement and change. The fire element is emotionally ruled through self-gratification and through generosity to others.

WILL YOU STILL LOVE ME TOMORROW?

One of the most important things that I have been recently working on and wish I could have shared with my younger self is to be clear and aware of what I am with my partner. Are we simply hooking up? Are we hooking up with casual dates on the side? Are we casual or are we in a relationship? Do we even want the same thing? Women usually need to know these things, but when we ask, it either comes off as being too abrupt or we simply don't ask at all. I have typically chosen door number two, much to my personal detriment. Neither are usually fruitful choices, unless you are one of those people who don't ask and doesn't care. I'll admit, sometimes, that sounds like a freaking fantastic world to live in. One of my friends, who's been a serial dater as long as I've known her, told me that the best lesson she's learned was to make sure the two people are both on the same page. Decide what you feel would be best on your end and have an easy-going discussion with your partner, friend, fuck buddy, whatever they are to you. Just make it clear at some point what road y'all are headed down. Too many of my girlfriends have gone out with guys, and have not been sure of what the hell they were. They sit by their phones waiting for some text that's probably not going to come in because the guy is not even aware that they want something more out of him.

TO SWIPE LEFT OR RIGHT...
THAT IS THE QUESTION

One night, after years of turning up my nose at online dating, completely over crushing candy (and at my girlfriend's behest), I caved and created a *Tinder* account for myself. I was very hesitant to even look at the app because I had always thought meeting someone should be an organic experience that would occur when it's meant to. My girls however, thought it would be fun and funny – which it had been- but it also was a very interesting and eye opening experience. After opening the app with hesitance (and some secret anticipation), I saw all sorts of pictures flash before my eyes as I swiped left, left, left, left, left, maybe right, then back to left, left, left. Even through all the giggling and expressions of shock and horror, my girlfriends and I were amazed at the shallowness or lack of awareness that these guys had. Did they not know, or care, that a camera was in front of them and that they were being judged simply by that picture? Did they think that smart women would want to mess with a guy who is wicked rude already in his bio? By the way, I have a handful of male friends who also have accounts and have shown me quite a few examples of the women that are on *Tinder*. Oh, dear sweet lord! What a hot mess that was! One guy friend in particular was pondering why women ask for a serious relationship on this app but then, post photos of themselves laying in their bed wearing practically nothing. I couldn't answer him.

There are all kinds of profiles on *Tinder* but the fact that it's how people are relating to one another, through this piece of technology, is quite a newfangled idea in my book. Do women expect to find a boyfriend or husband here? If they want to simply hook up, shouldn't they just go to a local club and pick someone up? At the same time, on these dating apps, you can narrow your search easier with settings like distance and age. In a sense, you're able to choose what you are looking for. It was a whole experiment I'm not sure I was ready for. There are a variety of obvious downfalls I found with this method. While one guy's picture might intrigue me, thanks to kind eyes and a nice set of biceps, if I meet him and he's dumber than a doorknob, we're in trouble. It's a bunch of blind dates that you have essentially set up for yourself, but pictures can be very deceiving. In an ironic way, it's a sort of old world method. Back in the days of old, no technology was available to transmit information quickly from one perspective partner to another; so, men of a certain social status would have to pick a wife by looking at their portraits. Now, as independent women, we are deciding our futures solely on pictures and 500 characters to go with them. I won't divulge names of the gentlemen (or fuckboys) that I went out with, but every experience was different. I met guys with all sorts of colorful backgrounds and personalities. What none of them were aware of was that I had done extensive pre-date research. I didn't want to get my ass *SVU'd*, so I always made sure to find out as much info ahead of time. Some dates shared their deep dark secrets willingly, like their drug habits, sexual escapades with celebrities, and even crimes they may or may not have committed. Others, however, failed to mention certain elements of their pasts, like being a former porn star, for example. I'm not one to judge a colorful lifestyle, a person's secret past is their business, but there is something to be said for me sitting there with this individual wondering when that small detail will come to light. Needless to say, this dude's secret remained his and it was a short-lived dalliance. There was another *Tinder* winner who started off on a very charming, polite and respectable note. Next thing you know, I'm at the car wash receiving photos of him cooking in the nude and asking me if I liked "a good bum." He then spent the next ten minutes texting me about how amazing his body was. Really bro? My car is dirty and we've "known" each other for four hours. I don't care.

While I may not have met Prince Charming yet (Ben Barnes is not on any dating app that I've found), I definitely have a variety of amusing stories and at the end of that particular journey… well, perhaps I'm not done? #swipeswipe

No, I think I'm good. *Tinder* is dead to me.

HERE COMES THE BRIDE?

"My marriage was over when I stopped laughing and didn't have shared experiences with him anymore."

ANNE F.

Some women marry out of love, others tie the knot for religious or financial security, but marriage is not for everyone. The history of marriage began as a business contract to unite bloodlines, kingdoms and very rarely, those in love. The fact that marital rape was legal in most states across the America until about 1993, when they banned it, is absolutely insane to me! That should tell you something right there about the mind-set of the people contracting marital unions for thousands of years. Marriage was not created for lovers, like we would all hope to believe, but getting married can have a beautiful side too. You are stating that you and another human being want to walk side by side in life together, and feel the joys and pains of the human experience no matter what; united in support and love. I would like to get married someday, (when my dream man, the talented actor Ben Barnes, heads this way, please let me know). However, I don't allow this want of matrimony to be something that consumes my daily existence or clutters my life. I have several girlfriends who don't want to be married or don't believe in it. They don't want the pressure that comes with a union that is fixed, or they want to have a career and life that is their own and not tied to another. Freedom is quite tempting to a strong woman with a fiery soul and big dreams; this I know first hand.

I do have many friends and family members though, who believe in marriage or are already happily (or unhappily) married. Either way, you cut the cake; I think all women feel the pressure sooner or later to be united in holy matrimony. It's a tradition that all societies know well, but young women everywhere need to start realizing that they do have a choice. Marriage in this day and age has become so revolutionized that it should not matter if you participate in all the hubbub or not. Most girls grow up wishing for prince charming to show up and then, realize later on in the game that there is no such thing. Even the most perfect partner will let you down at some point, as is natural for any human being. Expecting this perfection is killing our relationships, and we need to remember, that men, like us, are not perfect. The male species (and yes, I often feel they're a different species from women) needs help in understanding what women need in their relationships. Men are often much simpler creatures who operate very differently than we do. Don't get me wrong, many men can love very deeply, but are not typically reared with the same views of weddings and marriages as we women are from inception.

While doing my research and writing for this book, I interviewed several men of different ages and backgrounds. I wanted to know, from their perspective, what are things that women do that are annoying and/or frustrating and also, what do they love or admire most about women that is not a physical attribute? My findings were interesting and eye-opening. We can always learn things from the opposite sex.

> *"Women are all different but in general, they have preconceived notions as to how I am going to react to any given situation, no matter what it is, from visiting family to picking a travel destination. It frustrates me because I'm an individual, and I don't respond the same to every situation. I admire women's tenacity and their ability to think around a subject, even when there is a lot of stress and they are in the middle of it. Men usually lose their cool. Women can also procreate, which is something men will never be able to do. Without women, no one would be here."*
>
> **TONY, 62**

> *"What I find that I dislike in women is what I dislike in a majority of people. I dislike how indecisive women are. I am talking about big things all the way down to the small stuff. What I admire most about women is how powerful they are. I live with two women currently and some of the stories that they have to deal with when it comes to every situation is breathtaking. I hear stories from them about how some men treat them and how they manage to stay*

strong in the darkest of times, and it is truly something to admire and has inspired me to treat women better and not put them in those situations."

COLIN, 24

"I can't think of anything that truly annoys me about women, unless they have very high-pitched voices, but what I love and admire about them is their ability to be flexible and travel permanently. My wife and I have lived in four different countries due to my work, and my wonderful wife joined me on each and every adventure."

BEN, 81

"Women ask too many questions. Men keep it simple and generally don't ask each other directly what they are thinking. We are literally sometimes, thinking about nothing - we are defragging our hard drive… putting all the important shit in its place and filing it away. Too many questions= too nosy for many of us men."

ALEX, 38

"It frustrates me when you're dealing with an issue and women tend to have a lack of concentration on the subject at hand. Sometimes, their multi-tasking

abilities don't allow them to focus on just one thing at a time. You are trying to figure something out and they'll move on to something else before the first problem is resolved. However, there is nothing in nature and in the world that is more unique and perfect than a woman. I love that they are family-oriented and that they think and act more with their emotions which is a healthier way of existing because you're not suppressing everything- which is what men would be prone to do."

SOLEIMAN, 56

"What annoys me the most about women is that it is much harder for them to let things go and move past them. Not just grudges, but things that most guys would consider rather minor. I have always admired though, how women are able to multitask so well, and my admiration has only further strengthened since I've started working in production. In my experience, women are able to do a much better job juggling and keeping all the balls in the air."

MATT, 30

For those of you still in search of that perfect someone, it's great to know exactly what you're looking for. Be it a friend with benefits, a full-time lover or a relationship leading into marriage, make sure to be specific with where you want that arrow to land. I feel it's always good to make a list of your personal values and know what you want in a partner. Many girlfriends have recommended this practice to me and each time I've done it, I've found what I wanted on that list. A problem occurred though, when I realized only too late, the details that I left off the list, good or bad, were the issues I had with that guy. If you're serious about finding someone, your list should be serious; details truly matter. For example, if you're completely against smoking, then don't settle for someone who keeps a pack of cigarettes "only for when they drink." This habit will eventually irritate you so much and you will resent that person for it. What a waste of time on both ends. Being specific on what you're looking for is always the best practice. Make that list!

One of my aunties asked me a few weeks ago what was I looking for in a future partner, and I responded with a carefully thought out description of a very handsome man who has his shit together-emotionally, physically, financially and mentally. I told her I was not waiting on potential anymore, I'd been through enough boys and I wanted a man. She said though it was admirable to search for that, but I should not close the door on the possibility that there could be a partner out there who was beginning their ascent to the top as well. A man who wanted to build something together with his partner or be a supportive equal. Though he might not be at his full potential yet, he could be very close. She said, "Often, the ones who are already established believe that anything you accomplish or receive after you get with them was because of them." So, although that's not the case for everyone, it's not always your best bet to close the door because Mr. Right could be right in front of you, anywhere.

If you have a run in with true love, I say go for it. Though it may not be the person you ultimately end up with, though it may shred your ideas of happily ever after, hell it could break your heart in the end, it's worth it. There's nothing that can compare to the feeling of pure bliss for even those short moments together. Falling in love is not easy, it's not comfortable and certainly not for the faint of heart, but it's a life altering experience when it's real. You open yourself up to another and reveal your true vulnerable cravings, whether that love is returned or not. I can't say if it's a smart or foolish idea, but going through the journey that makes your heart soar to worlds unknown will change you forever.

The first time I fell in love, life stopped for me. Everything in my sphere just paused, balanced in this unknown excitement for seconds at a time. Then my attention would be brought back to reality, and a bittersweet yearning would set in. It was one of the most magical things that's ever happened to me, so far that is. It was not necessarily all fun; it was actually terrifying and didn't end well, but if I had the option, I would take that plunge again. The thrill and connection you feel when your soul meets up with an energetic match is purely electrifying lightning. Your life experience deepens when love takes hold; that, I can tell you, is priceless. No woman should have to go through life without knowing even seconds of true love, no matter what age it happens. Don't search for it. Allow love to find and surprise you. Leave your fears and preconceived notions behind, and follow the white rabbit into Wonderland.

My last (and most cliché) tip in this chapter is to keep an open mind. True love is completely possible, and can be lurking around any corner… sometimes a very unexpected corner. Now, while not all of you may have read Jane Austen in your lifetime, she had many insightful opinions on the interaction between men and women in her books, but let's face it, we're not in the 1800's anymore. If you miss your opportunity to dance with Mr. Darcy at the ball, you're not completely screwed. You can always secretly stalk him on social media. I know that's what I do… in secret, of course.

CHAPTER FIVE

NOTHING COMPARES 2 U

A chapter on heartache, loss and how to deal…

With what was said in the previous chapter, I now must continue and state the obvious: the heart is a delicate thing. It's a sensitive entity filled with energy, which is not always cared for properly. Others, or even the one who houses it, can hurt the heart, leaving it feeling weak and downtrodden. Often, we emotionally give what we are not to receive in return. Whether intentional or not, spurned feelings are the worst. Not everyone is meant to be together, and some matches are meant to be only for certain periods of time.

Through breakups we learn a lot about ourselves, about what we're made of and what we are willing to give up or fight for. Whether you've had great luck in love or not, in life your heart will be tested eventually by something, or someone. The goal must be to learn from the experience, then get back up and continue moving forward. Being the passionate person I am, I've had to learn throughout my life how to balance my emotions when it comes to something or someone I like. I found it difficult to be fully engaged when it came to an individual I enjoyed, without letting it take me over. Balance is especially important for a Gemini like myself, but sometimes, my heart just goes where it wants to.

We are women after all and no matter how much we want to protest against our natural tendencies, often, we can't help but think of the future. It's in our DNA, molded into our gender, to be curious as to whether that mate will provide what we need for our personal nesting situation. Men tend towards having one-track thinking, while women will multi-task the shit out of everything - and we are damn good at it. I find that struggles arise when, in the process of all of our busy multitasking, we get so far ahead of ourselves that we've already visualized our bridal colors and picked out our kid's names before we even hit our third date. I've never met a man who thinks that way, even if he is confidant the woman he's dating could be the woman of his dreams.

BOO...

I have found the clearest way to figure out what the fuck is going on with opposite sex is go by what a dear friend of mine says, "at the end of the day, people do exactly what they want to do, whether it's right or wrong." I go by exactly what the other party's actions are and try not to infer what I *believe* to be going on. Action expresses priority and one's actions will usually tell you more about their character than anything else. I know a lot of people these days don't like to face uncomfortable situations and instead pull shit like *ghosting* the person they were dating. For those of you that are not familiar with the term "ghosting," it's defined as "The practice of ending a personal relationship with someone by suddenly, and without explanation, withdrawing from all communication." As embarrassing and hurtful as it is, it happens to the best of us – it's happened to me. I know gorgeous and amazing women, and men, who it's happened to as well. It's just plain rude and cowardly. The disrespect and indifference you are showing another human being is just awful. Even in our fast paced society, with all the dating apps and whatnot, people deserve to be shown a common courtesy by letting them know the relationship is over;

it's the least you can do. Despite not liking awkward situations myself, unless I felt threatened, I would not do that to a person I had dated. If you don't want to date someone anymore that's your choice, but let him or her know so everyone can move on. Even a simple text will do! *Ghosting…* the coward's way out.

DON'T HOLD YOUR BREATH…

I know there's that one bad boy we all wish we could tame. Take it from me ladies, if there was ever a woman who used to loved bad boys it was me. He went to jail? Check. He's been in many fights (of course defending people's honor… right?) Perfect! His heart is wrapped 500 times over with shitty baggage? Love it. I know many of us strong women like the challenge, danger and thrill that this conquest brings, but I'm here to tell you don't hold your breath! While it's possible to have a Johnny Cash and June Carter situation, it's rare. Bad boys are that special breed of males that often don't grow out of their dark ways, no matter how mature they are. If you've made your wants and intentions known, will that guy walk that line for you? It's not that common, unfortunately, in this day and age. Or ever really! With that sad fact setting in, think about if that's something that you would really want. Spending every waking moment wondering if the lion you have wrangled will stay calm and sedated long enough to realize the truth of how amazing you are? I know it's tempting, but I would suggest removing yourself from those situations before they hurt you and waste your time. Bad boys are who they are and if it's meant to be, it won't be an eternal headache and heartache. But don't hold your breath!

If he goes on and on about how much he wants you and misses you, blah, blah, blah, but can't even be bothered to pick up the phone to call or text you, then let him go. He clearly does not want you in a way you would wish him to. Simple to say, but not always easy to do. Actions do speak louder than words. That is the most proven phrase. He may break your heart, the pain may damage your soul, but don't allow either to keep you down or waste your life. Somewhere out there, there is someone worthy of you and all that you have to offer. With the time and energy it will take you to convince yourself the fight is worth it to hang on to your bad boy, he may already be far down the road by then.

WHEN IT'S OVER...

When a relationship is over and done with, we are often told to respect ourselves. In my experience, after going through some very difficult breakups, I know I'm usually not in my body for a while, let alone able to respect myself. The tragedy of what's occurred is too intense to process and I have typically felt lost. Through this numbness, I've learned these do's and don'ts that I would like to share.

DO'S:

- Take time to heal your emotional wounds. Even the easiest of breakups take a toll and need to be processed out of your system before you move on to the next frog or prince.

- Hermit for a while. Sleep and meditation often help to bring you back to a safe neutral. Also, not having a ton of people constantly share their opinions of what you should do next is helpful. You need to be with you and you alone.

- Work out. The endorphins will help you to begin to process and push out the sadness and/or anger that has built up. Working out is one of the best ways to a clear mind.

- Allow friends and family to help you and care for you. As much as you think you can get through a tough breakup by yourself, it's not always wise.

- Keep busy. Sitting around thinking too much and replaying memories will only confuse your vulnerable mind. Find things to distract you and once you have eased into your new situation, you can face the demons of your past.

- Only eat when you feel you want to. Friends and family will try to keep us stuffed after a breakup but our internal systems may not agree nor want to be bogged down with tons of heavy food.

- Enjoy a bottle of wine, or two, when you want to. I don't believe anyone can judge your alcohol intake when a breakup is fresh.

DON'TS:

- Posting all over social media about how much your ex is a piece of crap and what he/she is all up to without you is tacky and makes you look very desperate. Plus, no one else cares - truly they don't.

- Playing games with your ex or their new significant other may seem tempting, but there is a reason you two are exes and messing with their current situation is childish.

- Don't shack up with the next person you see on the street. It will only confuse you and it's not fair to the other person. My suggestion is go to your nearest sex store, and buy the most durable vibrator they have. A vibrator will keep you busy, doesn't talk back and only requires batteries. Perfection. P.S. Sleeping with your ex's best friend is way too incestuous and an extra no-no. Don't do it!

- Live in sweatpants for a year and stop brushing your hair and teeth. Just because it's over doesn't mean your looks and hygiene should be sacrificed at the altar of carelessness.

- Drunk call or text your ex. It will only get messy. If you know you'll be drinking, give your phone to your most trusted friend and stay focused on the night at hand.

- Begin gorging and eating everything in sight. Eating in excess, out of depression or anger, will only wreck your body, internally and externally. It's not worth the 25 pounds you will have to work your ass off to drop later in life.

No matter how much we work at it, healing from heartache takes time. Though let's be real, even time doesn't heal all wounds. It's how to live with them and move forward in a healthy and productive way that matters. Have some self-respect in your love life and know when it's not meant to be. Love that's meant to be in the deepest, truest manner will come to fruition eventually. If that person loves you, there is nothing they won't do to protect you or that love, even if it means not having everything the way they want it. Though your heart may be scarred up, I think the more scars you have, the more of a pirate you've become. So, ahoy matey's! Let's move forward from the gloom and doom of suffocating heartbreak and find a way to live again. One day you will be able to look back and say to your past lovers with pride, something to the effect of "Look at what you lost, but more importantly, look at what I've become without you."

CHAPTER SIX

SELF DEFENSE & SELF-RESPECT

A real woman should be able to defend herself and those close to her. It's a patriarchal idea that women are meek and need a man to protect them. Though men tend to have a physical advantage over us, we women have been fiercely protecting ourselves since the dawn of time. Granted, it's very nice and comforting to feel protected by your significant other, but you can't always depend on that. Think of the mama bear that will protect her cubs with every inch of her being. All women have that fierceness within them. It's if (and when) we choose to bring that out of us that matters.

Think of all the tough women that faced the rugged west in the 1800s. They defended themselves, their families and their land while the men were off fighting wars or seeking more land and fortune. Many men also died, leaving their women to take up the business affairs as well. This is just a sliver of the long timeline of strong women getting shit done. Research your history and educate yourself on women who stood their ground and took care of business. Consider my personal forebears, the Scottish clanswomen who were fierce contenders, or the *Onnabugeisha*, who were upper class female Japanese warriors. There is also an Apache warrior named Lozen, who fought to protect her people and their homeland in the 1800s. The history books are full of women such as these to inspire and show us how important it is to know how to protect yourself and those you care for.

Whether it's guns, knives, a rape whistle or kick ass self-defense moves, be prepared and know what you are doing. Practice is so important! Pepper spray will be of no use to you if you freeze up and don't use it properly when an attack occurs. The more precautions you have taken and the more aware of your surroundings you are, the better you can protect yourself. If you are starting out from scratch and don't know where to begin, other than kneeing a guy in the groin, then here are some ideas for ladies of all ages to think about.

- Take a self-defense class and learn the sensitive areas on both sexes that can easily be injured and give you time to get yourself out of trouble.

- Know your rights within the law, so that if you do defend yourself with a weapon, you are still protected.

- Don't put your drink down in a bar. Though women hear this often, it's very important. It takes two seconds to drug a drink.

- If you're going on a first date, especially with someone you don't know very well, notify a friend or family member of your destination, just in case.

Another aspect of self-protection for women, and everyone really, is being aware of your surroundings. Living in big cities most of my life, this practice has kept me safe in the worst neighborhoods. Whether on the subway, out at a club, walking home at night, hell, even walking through Central Park in broad daylight - you need be attentive to the environment around you. Be aware of anyone following you or giving you odd vibes. Even those that act like they want to help you can often be predators. Keep your purse close, head held high and broaden those shoulders (we talked about this in chapter 2, remember?).

Your phone can also make you an unfortunate target. Scrolling though your social media or even checking emails for a minute can take your focus away from your surroundings. It only takes a second for your attention to wander and your guard to be let down. Murderers, rapists and crazy people tend to target easy prey; victims that won't see the attack coming. Have you ever watched *Law and Order: SVU?* Don't put your drink down when out socializing, don't fall asleep on the subway and no matter what, please don't walk down any dark alleys with your headphones on at night. You might as well go camping by yourself in the woods and turn your life into a horror film. Also, playing *Pokémon Go* by yourself outside a dive bar at 2am is strongly ill advised. Yes, I have been a witness to this. The girl literally had no idea what was going on around her. Yikes!

AN INVISIBLE PREDATOR

"Don't let anyone *ever* poison your honey," said my friend Jess, as she took my hand in understanding, when I revealed to her the recent emotional struggle I was beginning to process. Her words, spoken in confidence, struck a chord with me. I was hesitant to write this section of the book, aware that I would be bearing a hidden part of myself, but I felt it was important. I wanted to unabashedly discuss some of the struggles I have faced in a relationship wrought with emotional abuse. I felt it important to share some of my experience because if it helps even one woman or gives hope to those who've felt disempowered, it would be worth it. <u>You are not alone</u>.

Though I consider myself a strong female, I allowed emotional abuse to happen to me. I felt the words and bore the manipulations. Looking back at the twisted sickness I fell into, it makes me very sad. I would never be okay if one of my girlfriends stayed with a partner who called them *a whore, ungrateful* or *someone incapable of feelings*. So, how could I have stayed? I had been through shades of physical abuse in the past, but when it leaves a physical mark, people can tell. Emotional abuse often goes unrecognized because words don't leave a physical mark; they are easier to forget about and leave behind. Just because your partner hasn't thrown you to the ground or beaten your face to pulp does not mean you have not been abused. But when is enough, enough? When is the disrespect and misconduct of one that is supposed to be your partner in life and share in your most intimate moments recognized as a wrongdoing?

In my case, the abuse I suffered had a lot to do with issues in the bedroom and my career. Both topics

Chapter Six

created an outlet for my partner (at the time) to funnel guilt to me like it was no one's business. I was an actress and artist before I met this individual, so why it came as a "surprise" to him that I enjoyed my work and didn't mind the long hours is beyond me. He would proclaim, on multiple occasions, that he supported my endeavors and was my "biggest fan," however, when push came to shove, he was the first to complain that I never spent time with him and we never had sex. Allow me to clarify, we had more sex than any of the couples I knew. There is a point though, when a woman needs a bit of time to herself, and not everyone wants to have sex all day every day! God forbid I was not in the mood that day or night, the guilt and verbal punishment would then enter the bedroom like a silent serpent to prey upon my soul, and push me into accordance. I would hear comments like, "When we got together, you were so sexy, now you're just cold and boring. I'm going to get you drunk so you'll be fun for once," and "Why are we together if you don't care enough about my needs?"

On a more public note, I was in Europe on a film shoot and we were partying with the crew one night. On the way back to the hotel, and in front of several crew members, producers and actors, my boyfriend announced that he and another actor were going to find hookers. They then jumped out of the van, and he slammed the door in my face, laughing. Needless to say, I was beyond mortified, but bit my tongue and carried on while everyone stared at me. This is only a small glimpse into what occurred between us; but after the abuse escalated, several plates were thrown my way and he cheated on me with a stripper; I decided enough was enough and left this toxic situation. I know I made mistakes in this relationship, but I always wanted to grow from them, not harm my partner. Uprooting this past trauma now, has helped me to learn what I believe is acceptable behavior within my romantic relationships.

Abuse, physical or emotional, is not exclusive to a particular gender. It can happen to anyone. I urge you ladies to be there for one another and if you or a friend is struggling through something, ask for or offer help! I never spoke up about the abuse I sustained until months after my breakup; I not only felt weak, but also that I wouldn't be taken seriously. Looking back, I wish I had said something, been stronger, stood my ground and left earlier. Better late than never though. Disrespecting another human being should never be acceptable, and the moment we turn a blind eye to it, we are allowing it to be okay. I have my flaws, just as all humans do, but never again will I allow myself to sustain malicious abuse like that, just because I think I'm strong. If you, or anyone you know is going through shit like that or worse, be discrete but don't be silent. Women need to stand together. A powerful woman knows when the game is up and it's time to leave. Exiting stage right!

If you need/want further information
or help, please visit
The National Domestic Violence Hotline

www.thehotline.org

or call
1-800-799-7233 (24/7)

GILDING THE LILY

In this second section, we will discuss things like fashion, culinary expertise and money - things that truly can only add to an amazing woman's external character. From a sexy pair of heels, to financial independence, a lady should always be aware of how to adorn herself, whatever her fancies may be.

CHAPTER SEVEN

SCENT OF A WOMAN

"Where should one use perfume? A young woman asked. Wherever one wants to be kissed, I said."

-COCO CHANEL

When I was a child, my mother taught me that any rough day could be fixed with a good perfume. She introduced me to *Chanel*, *Dior*, Egyptian oils and so much more. Growing up, it wouldn't matter if she was rolling in the dough or only had $50 in the bank, my mother would always smell deliciously alluring without fail. Since my childhood days in the suburbs, I've learned to cultivate my own worldly taste in scents. I certainly no longer insist on mixing two different perfumes, hoping to spray away the pain of teenage angst. I also accept the fact that once a perfume hits my skin, it will mix with my body's chemistry and sometimes, it just doesn't work out. Not every scent will be cohesive with you, so I suggest you know that and learn what turns you into Aphrodite the minute that nectar hits your skin.

One of the women I interviewed for this book described perfume to me as "the unseen accessory," which I felt was perfect! Just like dressing well or having a nightly beauty routine that makes your skin glow, I feel it's important for anyone, female or male, to smell marvelous. Ladies love a man who smells nice; it's sensual, it's masculine; why should we slack when it comes to our own aromas? There is a magical aspect to one's own chemistry and scent, but when you add fragrance to skin, it electrifies the senses and takes those around you on a journey.

The history books state that the oldest perfumery, found in Cyprus, dates back over 4,000 years. From the ancient Egyptians to the men and women of the middle ages, the higher classes would use flowers, oils and spices to smell nice since a bath was not an everyday occurrence and personal hygiene was nowhere close to today's standards. Even their living quarters would need assistance in the olfactory department due to inevitable issues like chamber pots and general mustiness from the weather. Since the days of old, the production of perfume has evolved quite substantially, and yet its application still remains a true statement of refinement in humans, especially women.

For me, choosing a perfume depends on whom I may spend my time with; that determines what I will smell like that day. Different personalities respond in a variety of ways. If I know I'll be meeting with a businessman who wears *Hugo Boss* and *Armani* suits, I won't be piling on the patchouli anytime soon. For this meeting, I would choose a scent that mirrors his drive and hustle, but brings a bit of sweet mystery to the situation. If a woman chooses to wear a fragrance, it should be one that she loves, but also one that mirrors what the situation calls for.

The reasoning behind this idea is twofold. For any work function or red carpet event I attend, I always wear *Ellie Saab* perfume. There is something about the smell of this fragrance that hits my brain and says, "Time to turn it up, girl!" Perfume influences your own emotional and mental state, and can also serve as a subtle tool for seduction. Whether the seduction is sexual, professional, or platonic, the scent of your skin can arrest the minds of even the cleverest individuals. At the end of the day, a woman must wear the perfume for herself. An independent, elegant Hollywood actress once told me "Confidence and satisfaction with yourself are the ultimate attractors."

I've had scents made for me specifically, I've dropped a pretty penny in a Beverly Hills perfume boutique, and I've also been known to pick up a travel size *Victoria's Secret* spray last minute because I was on the road and didn't want to spend too much. So, I guess you could say I'm all over the map with my love for fragrances. The price of a stunning fragrance is inconsequential if the scent is truly appropriate for you, and makes you feel like the goddess that you are. In my opinion, perfume should release and enhance your inner essence, rather than mask a bad smell. If you are unsure where to start with your choice of perfume or are just looking for a new scent, you can always ask a salesperson for a small sample to take home and try. I have done this on several occasions and it's been very helpful.

To get you started, here are some of my best recommendations for several different vibes:

- If you want to provide a vibe of sensuality and flirtation, try scents like Zara's *Vanilla Wood*, which I discovered while in Europe and have continued to buy it since. Another winner is Yves Saint Laurent's *Black Opium,* which I fell in love with from a sample in a magazine, of all places. It's so sexy that my friends and I call it the "date perfume." Both scents are darker, but sweet, with hints of vanilla in both.

- If you enjoy the lighter side of life, I recommend *Florence* by Tocca, a sweet and innocent floral perfume that my sister discovered. She, my mom and I all fell in love with it instantly. You can purchase the Tocca line at *Sephora*. Another family favorite that somehow, my grandma, mom and I have all been wearing (odd) is Lancôme's *La Vie Est Belle*. I also have several friends that wear it and have never personally found a perfume that smells this delicious on such a variety of women.

- If it's the professional woman of action fragrance you are going for, the classic perfumes have been tried and true for decades and are often a good bet. While *Miss Dior* or Chanel's *Coco Mademoiselle* are my top picks, I could also recommend a newcomer, *Olympéa* by Paco Rabanne. If you are feeling adventurous, it's a fragrance created for the "modern day Cleopatra" and has an impressive mix of ingredients including hints of Oriental citrus, salted vanilla and cashmere wood.

- If you're a Coachella-going bohemian princess, you might like scents such as Elizabeth and James' *Nirvana White (For her)* or Tokyo Milk's *Le Petit*. Both have slight hints of patchouli, but are not overpowering.

WARNING: There is such a thing as too much perfume! You don't want to overpower the nasal cavities of those around you; some people are sensitive or outright allergic to scents. Others will even get migraines if a scent comes on too strongly. When you go in for an important meeting, jump on a plane or make a hospital visit, it's usually best to keep the smelling divine to a minimum or sometimes nothing it all. Instead, just be safe and opt for an appropriately pleasant body aroma. Also! Please note that not every guy wants his girl to smell like chocolate cake or vanilla pudding. While you may think sugarcane peppermint mocha perfume smells so good, think again. Chances are when you and your man are getting intimate, it's not food he's thinking about eating!

Beauty blogs, magazine articles and even my grandma taught me that the best places to wear perfume are behind the ears, behind the knees and the neck. Your hair can also be lightly sprayed, it will hold the scent for a long time. Apparently, even the belly button works for perfume, but I never get that crazy. Anywhere that holds heat is a great place to apply the scent.

It doesn't matter what she does for work, or where in the world she lives, the skin of a lady should be soft and inviting so that she and others may enjoy the complements of its true nature. I like to spray my perfume on right after a shower, when the pores are open and inviting. First, I will prep my skin by scrubbing it and then, moisturize with coconut oil while still in the shower. Coconut oil is so incredible and multi-purposed; you can use it for everything from a hair mask to lube. After showering and moisturizing with this gift from the heavens, dry off and just pat dry where you have moisturized; your skin should feel like silk. Putting fragrance on freshly washed skin is magical; the perfect feminine touch when getting ready for anything. Spritz your perfume of choice lightly, and enjoy the effects of smelling like the goddess you are for the rest of your day… or night.

A PYRAMID SCHEME

When you spray your skin with perfume, do you notice how initially it may have smelled different than what it has become 20 minutes, or even an hour, later? In the art of perfumery, there are three "notes" that come together, in a triangle shape if you will, to create the scent you smell. *Top notes*, *middle notes* and *base notes* are carefully blended together, all with individual purposes.

The top note, also known as the head note, is the first smell that hits you after applying the perfume. Top notes are typically light, uplifting and the first to fade from your skin. They are often fresh and buoyant scents like citrus fruits, berries, bergamot, or herbs like clary and sage.

The middle note, also known as heart note, will arrive just as the top note starts to evaporate from the skin-handy! Who knew your perfume was working this hard for you? The middle note is where your floral and spicier scents will come in; they are a bit softer and will hold to the skin a bit longer. Jasmine, rose, coffee and ylang ylang are common middle notes to be found in high quality perfumes.

Base notes are the grand finales to the grand production that is your scent. Cacao, amber, patchouli, musk and vanilla are just a few of the well-known bases that bring your entire scent together, and remain the longest on your tender skin. These scents are rich, full-bodied and give off that air of dark mystery that is truly appealing to the senses.

The creation of fragrances is an enchanting process that has only become more adventurous in modern times.

With technology and science constantly advancing, there are all sorts of perfumes out there. Like most words that originate from Latin, *perfume* comes from the phrase "per fumus," which means "through smoke." Lucky for us, we have come far from the ancient days when people had to pick, crush and boil to create their own concoctions. Everyone has the right to smell good and in my perfect world, everyone absolutely would!

CHAPTER EIGHT

HEY GOOD LOOKIN'

"I like being a woman, even in a man's world. After all, men can't wear dresses, but we can wear the pants."

-WHITNEY HOUSTON

When I was a child, and perhaps into my teens, depending on who you talk to, there was nothing I liked more than dressing up like a Park Avenue heiress and strutting around for everyone to see. I would make my sister, Chelsea and cousin, Haley, join in the fun as well. While I would be the leader of this extravaganza, their fashions were nonetheless stunning and over the top as well. This event typically happened in my house or at family gatherings, so my audience usually consisted of family and close

Chapter Eight

friends. I would collect costume jewelry and dresses to layer over one another, while tights and bedazzled items lined my draws awaiting a wedding or reunion where we three ladies could debut our newest over-the-top fashions for all to see. Some of you may be reading this thinking "this girl is cray," while others, who know me better, realize how little I've changed since those days. I absolutely adore dressing to the nines. My godfather used to tell me all the time "Alexandra, don't gild the lily," but listening to that advice has never been one of my strong suits.

Fashion may be subjective, but let's face it, most people can tell if a woman looks good and has it going on or if she's just a hot mess. Looking good is an idea that may not be appealing to all, but I find it very important. We don't need to walk around in red carpet gowns everywhere at all times, but I do feel that as a woman, you should be conscious of looking appropriate for where you are headed or what you are doing that day. No matter your style, looking put together denotes that you care and are aware of your own person. If you are off to the gym, you don't necessarily need a face full of makeup and a push up bra (you're at the gym to work on your #squatlife), but if you are headed to the bar for a date or even to hang out with the girls, don't wear sweats or forget to run a brush through your hair. Take pride in your appearance and get creative with your fashion. No matter what your style, remember that how you present yourself is how the world will receive you.

LESSONS FROM A JEWISH GRANDMA

You don't have to be a religious reader of *Vogue* to be concerned with, or even interested in, fashion. Each and every woman has her own idea of fashion and one of our perks is to be able to wear and appreciate a nice outfit… or two… or 50. If you can afford it, allow yourself to splurge once in a while, but know that no matter how rich you are, or may become, there is no shame in finding great deals in the clearance rack! YAAAASS QUEEN!

Clearance shopping is one of the best things my grandma taught me when I was young. She would take me to get new clothes a couple times a year because my mom loathed doing it; I guess it skipped a generation, because I adore shopping. The minute Grams and I walked into the store, she would pull out coupons and direct me to the clearance racks. If you have a little patience, know where (and when) to look, you can get amazing deals. When I go clothes shopping, I'll usually start in the sale area, which is typically in the back of the store. You can also check online to see if there are coupons or sales you didn't know about going on for that store. Save a buck when you can, it always pays off later;

money saved is extra sushi dinners in my book! Also, if an item comes out that you just love, it will probably go on sale in a couple of weeks, so you can always risk it and wait a bit. Stores like to move their products fast and styles are always coming and going, so be aware that you could be paying double now what it will cost you later. If you have patience, you can often eventually get it for a steal!

RULE #1

Dress for your body type. This is an unsaid steadfast rule in fashion. No matter your body type, the fabric covering it should be appropriately fitting. I cannot tell you the amount of times my retinas have been scarred by seeing a girl whose skirt is beyond too short and too tight, so much so that I see her crotch, panties and God knows what else is going on down there. Unless you're a dancer in a gentlemen's club and you are at your place of business, keep those bits private and don't give away the goodies on a street corner to all passing by. Muffin tops, butt cleavage and other wardrobe faux pas are easily avoided with proper fitting clothes, no matter how big, small or in between you are. Be realistic with yourself, if you're a size 6 then wear size 6, not 4. And vice versa, I never recommend that women wear clothing three sizes too big for them unless they are home sick and living on the couch.

LEGGINGS

I love leggings just as much as the next girl. Leggings are comfy, you can layer them and best of all, they always come in black. Amen to leggings! I must caution however, that if you want to wear leggings, please know that panty lines are a thing- and not a good one. When wearing any sort of tights or leggings, I suggest wearing a thong or wear a long enough shirt or tunic dress to cover the lines. Also, make sure that your leggings are thick enough so as not to show the color details beneath them. The last thing you need is for the world to know that you wore pink panties with hamburgers on them.

Last but not least, keep in mind that although extremely comfortable, generic leggings are not acceptable to wear on every occasion. The whole world is not your gym.

SHOES

Every woman should own at least one pair of heels; I don't care if you got them in Milan or at the *Goodwill* down the block. High heels extend the look of your leg, and I honestly think they are the most beautiful type of shoe. Heels take the line of a leg and turn it into perfec-

Chapter Eight

tion. When it comes to high heels, there is an amazing variety of designs, colors and styles, but you can never go wrong with black. There should be at least one pair of black heels residing in every woman's closet. They are as basic and necessary as owning a toothbrush.

Once you have your heels, make sure you know how to walk, run, skip, jump, have sexual relations or do whatever in them. If you don't know how, then practice. It is a HUGE pet peeve of mine when women put on a pair of heels and clunk around in them like a farmer coming out of a mud pit. Train yourself to walk in high heels. It's not that big of a deal, think of it as more of an art form. As I trained my four-year-old ballet students to say, "practice makes *perfect*!" Now I do have friends who say, "but Alex, they hurt so bad and my toes are crushed. I'm just gonna wear flats." My response has and always will be a shaking of the head "no," and a simple answer of "You just haven't found the right pair." Yes, we can all agree that after five or so hours, heels may not be the "most comfy". You are essentially wearing a device on your foot that shoves all of your weight forward onto the toes… but it just looks so damn good! We can usually laugh about it, but seriously, my girls better be wearing heels when we go out.

Keep in mind, not all shoes are going to be comfortable. Explore the shoe world to find out what your feet like, so you may search for a pair of decent heels that you can wear to a wedding or a funeral. With the exception of disturbing the body or talking on your cell phone during the service, there is nothing more disrespectful than showing up to a funeral wearing sneakers or flats. A person's passing is worth you suffering through a few hours in a nice pair of black heels. My friend Kendra will wear heels (which she doesn't love) when we go to events together like the ballet, or out clubbing, specifically because she knows she is going with me, not because she likes them. I think that it's beyond sweet of her to do this, but better yet, I'm glad when she does because she has a killer pair of calves and when they are utilized with a nice pair of heels, watch out world! Woot! Woot! On our last trip to Vegas for her birthday, Kendra in a nice pair of heels not only got us into VIP everywhere, but also attracted some major attention which came with free drinks and a fabulous time for all. Moral of the story is that a great pair of heels can take you places!

TIP!

If you are worried about blisters on your toes or feet in general, I do have a tip for you! Use something called *new skin* or *2nd Skin*. It is a dancer's secret and easy to purchase at any pharmacy or supermarket. Use it like nail polish and paint and apply a small bit of that stuff on the areas of your feet you're concerned about. Let the liquid dry before you put your shoes on. It literally forms a second layer of skin and protects the easily irritated areas that are the first to form blisters while partying the night away. Voila!

ABSOLUTELY *NOT* FABULOUS

HOUSE SLIPPERS ARE NOT APPROPRIATE FOOTWEAR TO HAVE ON YOUR FEET ANYWHERE OTHER THAN INSIDE YOUR HOUSE. That was the only way I knew how to get that point across. I'm talking about those people that wear their slippers out to CVS and the grocery store. It's such a no-no and definitely cannot be sanitary. You're taking shoes that are meant to be worn inside your house, and wearing them out in the world of stores, malls, subways and lord knows where else… disgusting and not ladylike. You might as well wear your sneakers all the time and save some money.

Although you don't wear them on your feet, the same thing goes for pajamas. Don't wear them anywhere but in your home! I don't know about other places, but growing up on the east coast in Massachusetts, I saw this shit happen all the time. I seriously cannot imagine what is going through some woman's head, when I see her at the gas station in her pajama pants looking as though she is wearing a normal, everyday, appropriate outfit. Once again, not sanitary! Are you sleepwalking? Are you the spokeswoman for your own pajama brand? Cause, if not, please wear some real fucking pants to the gas station.

Wearing socks with sandals is another common crime in fashion. It should be against the law and honestly, I feel like making the *Home Alone* face when I see this aberration. It makes no sense! Do your feet want to be covered, or don't they? Why would you do that?! Oh, and unless you're in the Alps climbing mountains with the Von Trapp family, clogs do not need to be worn. Ever. 'Nuff said.

CORSETS

Every woman would be well advised to own a corset, professional strength or not. It's that one piece of historical fashion that really served a purpose then and, very often, now. Today, you can find celebrities like Lily James, Amber Rose, Nicole "Snooki" Polizzi and the Kardashian sisters taking advantage of wearing a "waist trainer," which is essentially just a corset. Hell, today on my hike I saw three different women wearing them! Whether you wear it now and then, or use it regularly, a corset is great training for sitting up straight- if you didn't already spend 15 agonizing years of ballet with teachers constantly yelling at you to keep your posture. Because I grew up classically trained in ballet, I'm used to tight things around my waist and really feel comfortable when I wear a corset or bodice, but I also enjoy collecting them for my own personal closet of costumes. A corset is a fun and sexy costume piece for the boudoir as well! There is something about unlacing, unzipping, unbuttoning or unhooking a corset that leads its viewer to expect the world within to bring amazement beyond their wildest dreams. It's the mystery beneath the corset that drives some wild, while others love the look of a tapered waist and overflowing breasts to match. For women who were not blessed with a bountiful set of breasts, a corset is also a fabulous tool to heave those girls right up and create the ultimate and curvaceous cleavage. Ooh la la!

MAKEUP

In the spring of 1988, my mother awoke one morning to find my crib empty. Panicked, she ran through the house till she found her child (face down) in the bathroom, which was covered in red. She screamed, thinking the red to be blood and her child dead. With closer examination, however, my mother realized that her little Gemini daughter had maneuvered her way out of her crib and over to the bathroom. She then outsmarted the child lock and found her mother's makeup bag. The little girl had taken out the deep ruby red lipstick and smeared it all over herself, her clothes and the entire bathroom. That is a classic baby Alexandra story. I *loved* lipstick before I even knew what it was and I mean LOVED it. Fast forward many years later, I now lend Mumsy my red lipsticks quite often. So, we have somehow come full circle; it's quite comical.

Makeup, like perfume, is an ancient treasure that women have been lucky enough to indulge in for centuries. Whether using charcoal on the eyelids, or powdering the skin so fair with a lead-based mixture, historically, makeup has been known to alter looks, disguise flaws and enhance the stunning beauty of our natural selves. Today's application of this exterior accessory can be an interesting subject around women. Some women are very good at it, some are decent and some females have no idea what the hell they're doing.

What I find interesting is that, skin tones are obviously not all the same, and different cultures typically idolize different looks for their women. I have many Asian dance students who think my pale skin is stunning. They like to touch it and admire how white I always am. However, when I lived in Miami, I was practically the freak. Everyone around me was extremely tan or dark

Chapter Eight

skinned and I looked almost see through compared to them because of my fair skin. Everyone was always telling me I needed more sun or that I should use a tanning lotion.

Being in an industry that often revolves around how a person looks, I know many women who are very good at their makeup artistry. They know the difference between a foundation brush and an eyeshadow brush, and contouring is their specialty. I can honestly say, looking back at my relationship with it all, I didn't know what the hell I was doing with makeup as a teenager. I wasn't completely stupid, but I used way too much makeup and definitely did not highlight or contour. While practice does make perfect, if no one tells you otherwise, sometimes you don't know any better. Everything changed for me when I was 19 in New York City and met my amazing friend Amanda. Though we may have been students of the theater, this girl was a professional when it came to anything makeup, and she knew her shit. Amanda was the first person to help me rediscover my natural beauty and opened that Pandora's box, so to speak. I have never been the same since. Before my tutorials with her, I didn't know about eyebrow formation, primer, or even the proper application of under eyeliner. I was by no means horrible at makeup, although I'm sure she thought I was, but it was the application of it that was never my strong suite. When Amanda did my makeup, she would create these masks of color on my face that changed how I felt. My identity would transform with every stroke of her soft brushes. I would be decorated like my ancient ancestors had been before me, just with much higher quality products.

Makeup can be a very beautiful and creative way to decorate ourselves, but often, the downfall with it is completely losing sight (literally) of yourself. When too much foundation is packed on or eyebrows take over a face, I feel it can be detrimental to your actual beauty. I know some women don't feel comfortable or confident without ten pounds of makeup on, but I'm not a fan of that. For me, two products that have made a difference are primer and finishing spray. Primer is used on the face before applying makeup, while a finishing spray, or powder, is used after you're done and holds the makeup in place. I recently learned that you can also use rose water as a finishing spray. It's safer and healthy for the skin.

It's extremely important no matter how tired or drunk you may be, that you remove all makeup before you go to sleep. Your skin, sheets and possible bed partner will thank you for doing so. Be gentle around your eyes, as the skin is the most sensitive there. I love using coconut oil on my lashes to not only remove the last traces of mascara or eyelash glue, but also because it helps to condition the lashes afterwards. Again, yay for coconut oil! Castor oil can also be wonderful for your lashes, but it's much thicker and stickier, just FYI, so apply with a hint of caution.

Makeup can be a beautiful addition to your repertoire or it can be a cruel mask to conceal the truth. For me, it's a fun and creative practice that I'm constantly learning more about. I now follow makeup specialists online and through trial and error, I've really learned what colors and products work for my face. A huge thank you to Amanda for sharing your knowledge with a girl in need!

I will leave you with this thought: there's a time and place for cheap reddish pink lipstick. Never, and in the trash. Thank you.

JEWELRY

My grandmother once told me a woman should always have enough gold to flee the country. Granted, she lived in Egypt at the time and though that idea may be old school, it stuck with me. I do feel that all women should at least make it their goal to have some sentimental jewelry and gold - just in case! If the end of the world rolls around, you'll wish you had gold to trade for food. You'll thank me then, because trust me, you'll want to trade that instead of sex for items of necessity like tampons or toilet paper.

When it comes to basic everyday jewelry and accessories, there are many affordable ways to achieve a stylish look no matter the occasion. I have found that whether you're headed to the office, Sunday brunch with the girls, or even the club, stores like *Forever 21*, *H&M* and *Kohl's* are good bets. At these stores, you can find cute and super cheap items to flaunt. Worst-case scenario, if they break or you lose them, it's not a big deal because you didn't empty your bank account to make the purchase. During the creation of this chapter, I asked a handful of women what are six staple pieces of jewelry that every woman should own. Here's what it came down to:

1. A pair of classy diamond stud earrings and pearl stud earrings- they don't have to be real.

2. A great strand of pearls.

3. A sparkly statement necklace that can be worn with a fancy dress or with jeans and heels to spiffy them up.

4. A good (reliable, not necessarily expensive) set of hoop earrings, both in silver and gold.

5. A gemstone ring.

6. A piece that is sacred or special to the wearer. When she looks at it, she feels comfort, joy, safety; whatever the specialty of the piece may mean for her.

All professional jewelers that I have met strongly urge their clients to make sure they have a polishing cloth in the back of their closet. Jewelry should be kept polished as much as possible because it helps to keep the piece in better condition for a longer time.

NAILS

I learned at an early age how important a pedicure is. Dance is never kind to the body, but especially to the feet. I once had a nail lady tell me that back in Vietnam, they didn't have the fancy tools they have here in America and that they just used the concrete to scrape their feet. I asked if it worked and she said, "Of course it does. Cement is not elegant but it does the trick to make soft feet. You do what you have to right?" I smiled and agreed, but realized then that no matter what, my heels better be soft because concrete is everywhere, so I didn't have an excuse. It doesn't matter if you're a dancer, toll collector, or stay at home mom, take good care of your feet because they not only hold you up, but you don't want people comparing your tootsies to those of a hobbit or a gremlin.

My fingernails, on the other hand (hee-hee), have always been a challenge. My nails have been subjected to every option imaginable. When I was younger, I used to pick at them; so, in my teens, I decided to get acrylics, which of course weakened them further. I didn't care though because I wanted nails that looked like they were straight out of a music video. Since then I've had French manicures, gel nails, stickers on my nails and acrylics that looked like Atlantic city exploded all over them. Now, after all these years, I tend to keep my nails looking natural and get manicures when I can. Sometimes, in a fit of Gemini boredom, I will switch it up for a full set of subtle, but gorgeous, acrylics and just prepare to do damage control when I eventually take them off. I've found some helpful things for growing my nails that are actually quite simple.

- File often: The more you file your nails, the faster they will become healthy and continue to grow. I learned this tip from the only woman I've met working at the DMV who wasn't a bitch. She had the most amazing nails I've ever seen in real life. I mean academy award winners!

- Try some Biotin: It's a water-soluble B-vitamin that is helpful for your hair, skin and nails- WARNING: DO NOT OVERDOSE!

- Use a clear strengthener polish: Some options are better than others, so do your homework.

- Keep a healthy diet: The growth of your nails depends heavily on what you're putting into your body, so be aware of chemicals and additives in your food.

- Don't smoke cigarettes: In this day and age, it should go without saying, but I'm saying it again. Smoking can discolor and weaken the nails and is, in general, a disgusting and dangerous habit.

REQUEST!

No matter the state of your nails, please, please, please don't let your nail polish chip and then leave it there. Nails start looking like shit when they have old polish that's been picked at for far too long. It's not attractive, and we are not 12 anymore in the pool at summer camp. There is this thing geniuses invented back in the day called *nail polish remover*; use it! You can get it at the dollar store, so there is no excuse. Also, it can't be healthy to never let you nails breath. Let them breath

I've always found that no matter who you are, or whom people believe you to be, beautifying yourself should be a ritual about you and *for* you. From the scrubbing and shaving, to assembling an outfit and makeup choices, it should be a process that you enjoy and make your own. Whether you are a woman who loves a good milk and honey bath, or you prefer to wear your dreads with pride, take your routine and let it nurture you. It's your time and no one knows how to do it but you.

I will finish by stating that style is an overall expression of us and, as women, we should utilize every inspiration and whim we have to create outfits that make us feel our best. If you gained anything from this chapter, then I hope you will think twice before just "throwing something on," and heading out the door. Be creative and pick styles that make you feel the most comfortable. Allow vibrant colors and patterns to enhance your mood, but always remember, black will NEVER go out of style.

CHAPTER NINE

LA COCINA

Cooking is a flavorful art form that everyone should partake in at some point in life, especially women. I say this not because our purpose is to serve others, but because food is a daily part of our lives that nourishes and assists in our well-being. Both genders should know how to cook, plain and simple, but I have met too many women in the past couple of years that didn't know how to cook at all. You don't have to be Rachael Ray in the kitchen, but I really have a hard time respecting or relating to a woman who can't fry a basic egg or follow the simplest recipes. Your lack of knowledge in the kitchen shows me that you never took the time to learn this basic, functional skill of domestic survival. The ability to prepare food can be a joyful task that in many cultures is passed down through the generations. As my dear friend and mentor,

Chapter Nine

Carolyn, once shared with me, "... while take-out can be fun, curried potatoes and lentils over basmati rice or fusilli with baby-peas and black truffle oil are only two of the myriad of fab alternatives to spending hard-earned dollars at an upscale eatery." I typically find out that today's younger generations think using a microwave is "cooking." Here's a news flash for y'all: no child, niece, nephew, friend, husband, lover or boss of yours is going to want microwaved anything at your next sit down dinner.

While I'm aware that women have been sequestered inside kitchens for hundreds of years, I don't focus on that when I'm cooking. Being able to cook should not throw you into indentured servitude, unless you let it. I have so much fun cooking up a storm when I know that those I prepare food for will appreciate and hopefully enjoy it. I grew up with my father as the main chef of the house; he taught both my sister and I how to cook. This showed me at a young impressionable age that both men and women should be familiar with aspects of the kitchen. Now an adult, I love a man who cooks and somewhat expect it. It's very sexy and shows me he has skills and can care for himself - he's not putting his hunger level in the hands of another.

Now sometimes even the best of us will be way too tired and/or lazy when we get home and don't want to cook. I feel that way often these days because of my busy schedule, so in those instances I get creative! I don't just pop in a frozen dinner or drive to the nearest fast food stop when there are so many culinary experiences I may not have tried yet. I am still surprised at the amount of people I meet that have not eaten sushi- it's 2017! Where have you been? I understand raw fish may not be at the top of your food wish list, but have you ever tried authentic Greek, Vietnamese *Pho* or a nice prepared Caballero steak from your local grocery store's prepared food section?

Another option for you busy hotties is to prep your food at the beginning of the week. I have many friends who train hard core at the gym and have very specific diets they must stick to. These dedicated females prep their meals on a Sunday night, cooking up a healthy storm and then section it out in portions and shelve it in the fridge. While meal prep may not quite leave your options open for what you'll be consuming during the week, it does help if you are working towards a fitness goal and don't have a personal chef available. Now that's dedication!

FOR THE DRINKERS OUT THERE

Anytime you go to a party, head out on a date or are just having a casual night at home with friends, *know your drink*. This trial by error knowledge usually takes some time and sometimes several nights of ending up on the bathroom floor to really learn what types of alcohol are your friends and which will unleash the demons inside. It only took me a couple of bad nights to realize that as much as I love country music, I'm most definitely not a whiskey cowgirl. A distinguished lady learns to not just order what the rest of her party is having but instead, drink what she truly prefers and knows.

Though you don't have to be a sommelier to enjoy a nice Chianti or Tempranillo (my personal favorite) when you form your own opinions of wines, or beers and liquors, your time spent drinking will be much more enjoyable and purposeful. People are also often impressed when you know a fact or two about what you're drinking. For example, how it's made, the history behind it or a unique twist on the recipe. So, get to know what you enjoy drinking most while out on the town or in the comfort of your home. There is much more to drinking than just getting your buzz on.

LET'S GIVE IT A GO

Moving back to food, if you have little to no experience in the kitchen and are not like Julia Child, who could afford expensive cooking lessons, here are some basic recipes I was taught that are simple but very tasty. I try to use only organic ingredients when I cook because they are healthier for your body and always make your dishes taste better. All these recipes have 10 steps or less. You can do it!

Measuring terms to know while prepping:

    tsp.   = Teaspoon
    oz.   = Ounces
    tbsp.   = Tablespoon
    A pinch = Literally just take a pinch

BREAKFAST:

Pancakes
Ingredients you will need:

- 1 cup flour (white, spelt, or a mix of the two)
- 1 tsp. baking powder (aluminum-free)
- 1-1/4 cup milk
- 2 large eggs
- A pinch of nutmeg
- 2 tbsp. butter
- 1/2 tsp. cinnamon
- 1 tsp. vanilla extract

Chapter Nine

Tools you will need:

Fry pan or griddle
Ladle (type of cooking spoon)
Spatula (also known as a turner, flipper, etc.)
Whisk
Medium / small mixing bowls, preferably glass or steel
Set of measuring cups and measuring spoons

1. Take the medium mixing bowl and whisk together all of your DRY ingredients.

2. Add the milk, vanilla, eggs in your smaller bowl and gently whisk until everything is mixed in well. The liquid should be a golden color.

3. Melt the butter in a saucepan over a LOW flame and then whisk into your bowl of liquids.

4. Now add the liquids into the dry ingredients bowl and mix together with your whisk for about a minute until smooth. Get your ladle and pick up some of your batter and pour it back into the bowl; it should have a smooth consistency.

5. Get out your griddle or fry pan and heat over medium flame for about 2-3 minutes until water (dripped from your fingers) sizzles when it hits the pan.

6. Add a 1/2 tbsp. of butter or coconut oil to your griddle to act as a lubricant and flavoring, even if it's a non-stick pan. If it starts to smoke, turn your heat down a bit. Your griddle should be hot, but not causing much smoke. Then, ladle enough batter to make about a 4-inch wide pancake onto your pan. A 10x10 griddle should make about 4 pancakes at a time.

7. When bubbles form on your cake tops, time to turn them over. Give them about 1-2 minutes and then remove from the griddle. Test the first one by cutting it open with a fork. The pancake should be fluffy not wet.

Making these will take some practice at first, so be patient with yourself. Once you get the hang of it, you can always add yummy additions like berries, chocolate chips or even bacon bits!

APPETIZERS:

Need quick and healthy options for appetizers? Here are two.

Santa Fe Salsa
Ingredients you will need:

1 16oz. jar of salsa (to use a base, basic brands are fine)
1 bunch of cilantro
1 bunch of scallions
2-3 cloves of fresh garlic [not powder]
1 *Roma* tomato
1 can of *Hatch* whole green chilies
1 tsp. cumin
2 limes
Fresh ground salt & pepper

Tools you will need:

Metal or glass mixing bowl - medium size
Large cooking spoon
Sharp butcher knife
Cutting board
A metal teaspoon

1. Pour the jar of salsa into your bowl.

2. On your cutting board, take one clove of garlic at a time, place the side of your knife blade on top of the clove and firmly whack it with the heel of your hand. Your clove is now smashed and easy to peel. Chop all three peeled cloves into thin slices and add to the bowl.

3. Rinse the scallions and cilantro very well to remove dirt and grit. Chop 2 of the scallions into small bite size pieces, and chop the leafy

tops of cilantro about the same. Add both to your bowl.

4. Trim the ends of the tomato off and slice length wise in half and each again so you have quarters. Take 2-3 sections at a time and slice across their length into bite size pieces. Add to your bowl.

5. Now slice each lime in half width ways (along it's equator), then over your bowl insert the tip of your teaspoon into the pulp and rotate the lime with your other hand, allowing the juicy goodness to drop into your bowl. Repeat with the other 3 sections of lime.

6. Add 2 of the Hatch chilies sliced sideways into thin strips, to your bowl.

7. Finally, add the cumin and then salt & pepper to taste. Stir your bowl for a minute and begin to smell the power of your cooking. Then a taste test! Voila!

Tuscan White Bean Dip

Ingredients you will need:

1 (15 oz.) can of cannellini beans, drained and rinsed
1 large garlic clove
2 tbsp. fresh lemon juice
1 tbsp. grated lemon rind
2 tbsp. extra virgin olive oil
1/8 tsp. sea salt
1/8 tsp. freshly ground pepper

1. Combine all ingredients in a food processor and process until blended.

2. Pour into a decorative bowl and drizzle with some olive oil.

Optional:

Garnish with a sprig of fresh rosemary or parsley.

Serve with toasted spelt toast points (easy recipe below) or baby carrots.

Toast Points

1. Toast 3 slices of sourdough spelt bread or some other yummy seeded bread.

2. Slice in an X formation, creating toast points (4 per slice)

3. Drizzle each piece with some organic olive oil and sprinkle with course sea salt.

MAIN COURSE:

For all you meat eaters out there, try this simple chicken recipe to impress even the foulest of guests… yes, that was a pun. I'm *that* good.

Roast Chicken Dinner
Ingredients you will need:
- 1 organic whole chicken
- 1 package of rosemary
- 1 package of sage
- 1 lemon
- 1/2 cup of olive oil
- 2 tbsp. sea salt
- 1 bag of carrots
- 1 sweet onion
- 2-4 shallots
- Pair of oven mitts

Tools you will need:
- Roasting pan without cover
- Pair of tongs
- Meat thermometer
- Serving platter

Chapter Nine

Chef knife

Turn on your oven to 350 degrees.

1. In a clean sink, open your chicken and throw away the bag of giblets inside.

2. Wash the chicken (inside and out) for 1-2 minutes under cool running water. This rinses the cavity and freshens the chicken for cooking. It's been "cooped up" for a while in there! Let the bird drain for a few minutes while you cut up the veggies.

3. Peel the onion and shallots and cut away all the ends. Then cut the shallots in half and cube the onion into 4 pieces.

4. Cut the tips off both ends of 6 carrots and cut into pieces no larger than your pinky, then again in half lengthwise.

5. Your bird has a large opening between its legs. Take about half of the sea salt and with your hand carefully rub the inside of the chicken. Watch out for sharp bone edges!

6. Now cut the lemon into quarters and squeeze 2 of them to rub/coat the inside of the bird where you just used the salt. Your bird is now

clean and smelling fresh! Toss those two lemon pieces out and squeeze the other 2 lemon's wedges inside and leave them there.

7. Add 6 leaves of sage and 2 stalks of rosemary to the bird's insides as well.

8. Put 2 tbsp. of olive oil in the center of your roasting pan, spread around by placing the chicken (flat side down, breast up) in the pan and wiggle it a bit. Rub some of the olive oil on top of your bird with your fingers. Then lightly salt and pepper the whole bird.

9. Place the veggies you cut up all around your chicken and drizzle the rest of the olive oil on them.

10. Using the mitts, place your bird into the 350-degree oven for about 1 hour and 45 minutes or until the meat thermometer reads 165 degrees when placed in a thick part of the meat under the breast.

When done, take the pan out and place on the stovetop to rest for 10 minutes or so. With your tongs, move the veggies to your platter, leaving room in the center for your bird. Then place the tongs inside the bird using your other hand with a fork stuck into its opposite end, lift the bird and place on your platter.

Carefully carve and serve your bird. Enjoy!

DESSERT:

This recipe is a bit more challenging but well worth it if you like sweet.

Apple Cheesecake/Tart
Crust:
- 1 stick of butter
- 1/4 cup of sugar
- 1 cup of flour
- 1 tsp. of vanilla

Topping:
- 2-3 apples (*Cortland* for sweet or *Granny Smith* for less sweet)
- 1/8 cup sugar
- 1 tsp. ground cinnamon
- Filling: 1 egg
- 8-ounce package of cream cheese
- 1/4 cup of sugar
- 1 tsp. of vanilla

1. Preheat oven to 425 degrees

2. Put all the **crust** ingredients in food processor and process until ball forms, approximately 20 seconds.

3. Press dough into a tart or quiche pan.

4. Put all the **filling** ingredients in food processor (there is no need to clean food processor since the ingredients are nearly the same as the crust) and blend until smooth.

5. Peel and slice 2-3 apples. Lay apples on top of filling in concentric circles.

6. Mix sugar and cinnamon and sprinkle over top of apples.

7. Bake at 425 degrees for 10 minutes, and then reduce temperature to 350 degrees and bake for 25 minutes.

The tart is done when the outside edges are golden brown, and the filling has puffed up and set.

IMPORTANT NOTE: We must remember that Julia Child did not begin cooking until she was in her thirties, so it really doesn't matter how old you are when you start your learning adventure!

Chapter Nine

The foreseen challenges in cooking could be not feeling skilled enough, not understanding certain terms in the recipes, or even hating the aftermath clean up. All of these roadblocks can be easily worked through, even if you find cooking not to be at the top of your list of interests. The best way to learn how to cook is to simply do it by trial and error. Cooking is not for everybody, but it's advisable to have some basic knowledge of it. Also, don't be afraid to use helpful tools like *YouTube* video recipes or *Google* searches to show you the proper methods and techniques.

Above all, whether it's a tray of multi-colored macaroons or a simple salad, have fun and enjoy what you cook! When you prepare food and feed people, you are nourishing not only their bodies, but their souls as well. With even basic cooking knowledge, you are able to appease not only your own appetite for zest and variety, but also the hungry tummies of friends, family and lovers alike. As for lovers, pick one recipe that will have them eating out of the palm of your hand, which may, in turn, inspire them to do so elsewhere. So, put on your funky apron, find some great tunes, open a bottle of something and enjoy the magical powers of the culinary arts!

CHAPTER TEN

BITCH BETTER ~~HAVE MY~~ MAKE HER OWN MONEY

It amazes me, although I know it shouldn't, that even now, in 2017, wages are not equal when it comes to males versus females for the same type or amount of work. I know I'm not the only person, male or female, who is outraged by this fact. The money issue between the sexes in the workplace is that under-the-radar itch that women are now really, *really* starting to scratch and pondering why this has not been fixed. I know we touched on this topic of equality in the beginning of the book, but seriously, if two human beings are doing the exact same job at the same talent level, then why is the paycheck for one sex higher than the other? You can find multitudes of articles, videos and interviews, with women, who are now speaking out about how wrong this is. This past year alone, Jennifer Lawrence, Emmy Rossum, Jessica Chastain and several other female celebrities are among the many women who have begun to fight for higher or equal pay rates as their male co-stars and that's only in the entertainment industry! Imagine what's occurring throughout the rest of the industries. I absolutely commend those individuals who're standing up against this outrageous injustice. It's ridiculous and unjustifiable, but what it all really boils down to is RESPECT. Aretha Franklin sang it best. If there is no respect for other humans, there is certainly no justice or even thought of equality.

In my mind, there is nothing quite like a woman with an immense drive to hustle and succeed. Some women do it effortlessly, some not so much. Either way, I'm still amazed by the strong women I come in contact with. I have girlfriends that are single mothers, foster kids, immigrants from war-torn countries, abuse victims - the list goes on. You'd never know those were the cards these ladies were dealt in this life because they don't let it define them. These women decided what they wanted and fought for it every day. It comes down to two simple questions: how bad do you want it and how far are you willing to go and fight for what you want? No matter the family, lovers, friends or pets that come in and out of our lives, at the end of the day, all we have is ourselves. Find that hustle and drive and run with it! Work while others sleep, keep focused when the naysayers tell you you're ridiculous. Most importantly, always have clear goals.

I don't understand females who don't know what they want to do with their lives. Don't you have any passions or interests at all? You can always change your mind, while ebbing and flowing through different areas of interest, until you find the right one, but have some interests. I knew that I wanted to be a performer since I was three and there was no doubt in my mind, but that's not always common. Since then, the details of my career have changed, but the goal remains. I recommend to young women out there, everywhere, to have ambition and know your objective. Without targets to aim and hit, no matter the size, you can become lazy and that is a form of self-sabotage.

Self-sabotage has run rampant throughout the generations. I hear it all the time in the young female students I teach dance to. I hear it from friends and even from my family. They say things like, "I'm gonna fail, I know it," or "I definitely can't do that," and as soon as I hear that, I tend to agree with them because if that's what's in your mind, then you're pretty much screwing yourself.

You have already set yourself up for failure, haven't you? Often, my students will say this because they don't want to be different from their peers and stand out. I always remind them that if you're good at something, then be good at it and take pride in it. I often hear my girlfriends self-prophesying that they will fail, their situations will be grim or that they are simply not worthy. WTF is that? I understand feeling self-doubt, but ladies, you won't get what you want in this life without pushing past your self-defeating attitude. I believe that this positive mindset must start young. Women need to be taught from a young age that they are worth something, that they matter.

CALM IT DOWN... CALM..IT..DOWN

Ladies, it doesn't help our cause when we get so offended by everything and everyone. The more we complain or start fussing about the littlest things, the more men look at us, sigh and chuckle. The more we complain, the less seriously they take us. You want equality between the genders? Then don't sit around whining in your book club that your husband doesn't think you will make a good politician. Go out there and make it happen! Demand that respect you have earned in a fierce but calm manner. When the request becomes more of a complaint filled with drama, people start to turn their ears off and just blankly stare. It won't get you anywhere. So, make yourself heard by being firm and taking action. Know when and where drama is appropriate; we are all entitled to bitch now and again, but pick and choose your battles if you want to be taken seriously.

No matter if life handed you diamonds from the beginning or a sack of shit, where you go next is your choice. As every day passes, know that you're the creator of your own destiny. No matter how much you want to push back against this idea, it's true. It took me years of stubbornness to accept that this was indeed a reality. If you want that promotion and it's meant to be, then you will get it, but your energy must be focused and clear. If you set yourself up for your goal, and have the talent to back it up, it will happen. If it doesn't pan out, then it wasn't correct for you and you need to change gears and move forward with a different plan.

Change is good because it gives us room to grow and explore possibilities we might never have thought of.

SEX & MONEY

In life, nothing is for free. Sex and money mix the way a handful of prescription pills and 10 shots of strong liquor mix; it can sometimes be fun, so I've heard, but overall, a wicked bad idea that's not without cost. I had an ex who thought he owned me. To this day, he still believes that everything I accomplished while with him was his doing because of the money we spent and shared during our time together. Nobody had a gun to his head. He had his free will and it was his choice to share his resources with me. This individual never had a problem with sharing money, until I left him, at which point he threw a tantrum, which lasted *way* too long. It's a shame that he never appreciated all that I gave to the relationship; emotional, financial or otherwise. When you give something, do it with a happy heart or don't do it at all. My mom taught me that years ago and it has stuck with me. If you give something, don't expect them to treat you like you are the grand duchess, you did it because you *wanted to*. Take responsibility for your choices and what you have given. I was always appreciative of what my ex shared with me, but if I could go back and do it again, I would do it differently. That relationship taught me that a woman should ALWAYS have her own finances, no matter what her partner says.

Through our years together, I eventually quit working to start my company, I spent all my savings and trusted that the love we had between us and the life that we were building together was enough. Clearly, it wasn't. The day I woke up to this realization, was the day I discovered how fucked I truly was. To add insult to injury, I also had to face the fact that I had essentially done this to myself. No matter how independent I'd thought myself to be, I had let my love for this partner blind me, and I ended up with nothing of my own except some family treasures, my clothes and a big financial mess (one that I'm STILL paying for today). I may have left his ass, but he left me with a large debt he swore had nothing to do with him. Instead, he listened to his "friends," who knew nothing of what we had been through as a couple, resulting in him only helping to pay a measly portion.

The same man-child I referred to in chapter 1, has a saying, "All women are hookers." Despite my absolute disgust with this, what he meant was that men will always have to pay for women, in one way or another. I understood his reasoning but never could agree with the idea because *hooker* is a job title and *women* are a gender. I lay at least half the blame for his distasteful notions about females at the feet of the women who have been in and out of his life. Women must realize that *we* set the stage and need to let men know how to both talk to us and treat us.

Clearly, the man-child's mother failed, especially in that department; but that doesn't leave him blameless for his belief system. In general, men are raised to believe that they must provide for a woman, or that women will only pay attention to them when they have a good job and lots of money. The truth of the matter is that times have changed; although it's nice for a man to be financially stable, we should expect the same from ourselves.

If you aim to start a family with someone, plan on (and expect) huge changes within your financial world. Obviously, children are expensive and typically finances will be pooled to raise them. But always remember, that money is family money and you should still keep an account for yourself. It has been suggested to me, more often than not, that *his, hers* and *ours* is the best way to go financially speaking when it comes to raising a family.

BUSINESS AND RELATIONSHIPS

No matter how well you get along with your significant other, starting or running a business together is usually a no-no in my book. It's too close to home and can become very messy when the gloves come off and the shit hits the fan.

Business is already a tricky beast to master, but when you add feelings and relationships into the mix, the complexity of who's top dog in your work pyramid can only escalate.

No matter their intention, harsh words that you would normally brush off in a business setting are not always easy to hear when they are coming from the one that shares your bed. If your business struggles, the pressure is on and when the going gets tough who do you usually lean on? Your significant other. Chances are, it's probably not an easy thing to do when you're running a business together and sharing the same struggles. It's difficult to distinguish where the business ends and the relationship begins. Even though you may understand and love one another, this type of partnership isn't for the faint of heart. Is it worth risking that love? If all were to crumble, you would not only be losing your business partner but your lover as well. Just save yourself the time and agony and don't do it. If you do happen to go down that road, put on your seat belt!

DON'T KNOCK IT 'TILL YOU TRY IT!

I'll tell you one thing, never underestimate the power of a housewife. Whether she has children or not, keeping a house tidy and functioning is no small feat, especially if she has no help. As I was mopping floors and washing mirrors yesterday, like a scullery maid, I realized my mind was thinking of five other things at the same time, but it didn't make the labor any harder or easier. I was just going through lists in my head of groceries that needed to be purchased, plants that had or had not been watered, dry cleaning to be picked up and much, much more. And I couldn't stop it!

Now multiply that by a bunch when you add kids, their school, a husband, your own life, etc. Being a housewife is, in itself, a full-time job. It means being capable and available to cook, clean and take care of all the details pertaining to the running of the household and everyone in it. Props to those ladies! While that may seem silly to some, don't knock it till you try it. At different points in my life, I've lived in a tiny closet apartment with broken windows and a spray-painted bathtub, a suburban split-entry, and a six-bedroom house in the Hollywood Hills. No matter where I was, I maintained the household and it was always a never-ending task. Like most children, while growing up I did not understand what it took for my parents to keep a roof over my head, healthy food on the table and the toilet clean. My mother worked especially hard to keep the household running, while working lord knows how many jobs. I now look back and realize the amount of energy that woman put into sustaining a nice home for us. I am beyond grateful for her teaching me to appreciate those who care for the home as a main focus.

D.I.T.

In modern day filmmaking, there is a position behind the scenes entitled "D.I.T," which stands for *Digital Imaging Technician*. This person takes the footage and transcodes it so that it may be organized easily for the editor. However, this book is about women, not film, so this section is called D.I.T. for another reason.

It means "Do it today!" Meaning, get that shit done today - not tomorrow or the day after. Today! I bring up filmmaking because I often think about the slew of nights, including last night that my producing partner and myself have been up until four or five in the morning just to figure out how to get something done for our edit or current project. It could be as simple as transcoding a piece of footage properly, but neither of us went to film school, so any bit of our filmmaking tutelage came from either learning from our mistakes, or simply searching for the answer and figuring it out on our own. We didn't want to wait and spend unnecessary money to hire someone if we could figure it out and get it done right there and then. While many times our stubbornness has not served us, I think this practice does showcase our strong work ethic and the rewards are always sweeter knowing how hard we fought for them. It has also been a blessing when we've hired people that turned out to be idiots and could not complete the task at hand, despite being on our payroll. Thank goodness we learned how to do so many jobs behind the scenes. It comes in handy!

Chapter Ten

The women that inspire me the most are the ones that are fierce about realizing their dreams and going after them. I admire women with the will to persevere, figure out what they don't understand and broaden their educational horizons, without waiting for others to hand it to them.

Sometimes, the frustration of not knowing what the heck you are doing will drive you insane, but stay focused and keep teaching yourself new things. My girlfriend Natalia is one of these young women who has urged me to teach myself new skills. She will stay up as long as it takes to complete her tasks, whether she knows how to do it or not. Natalia runs her own successful fashion line and has built the business herself, from the ground up. From dressing A-listers to organizing accounting for the business, this badass often takes matters into her own hands. And speaking of hands, half the time I see her, Natalia's hands are stained with dyes and who knows what else from the shenanigans she's been meddling with to dye her groundbreaking metallic knitwear. It's awesome! She didn't wait for someone else to coach and guide her, the success has been mainly Natalia from the beginning. There, of course, have been multiple people who have helped her along the way but that's because they trusted her talents and her will. Dream big ladies, get out there and do it today!

We are so blessed to live in an age where we are able to find almost anything out with the touch of a screen or type of a key. The internet has opened up a whole new world for people everywhere, in which they have access to educating themselves more readily than ever before, so take advantage!

CHAPTER ELEVEN

WOMEN OF INSPIRATION

During one of my years in theater school, our voice and dialects teacher had us memorize John Keats' *Ode on a Grecian Urn*. Mastering this piece, written in 1819, was an event unto itself, not only because we had to do it in one night (and there are five stanzas), but also because the language was so intricate. It was important to make sure the poem's meaning came across in our precise delivery. *Ode* provides a haunting, yet carefully mapped out look at the beauty and depth of what this urn represents; a history and unique beauty that should be cherished because it will eventually fade and be no more. I bring Keats' cherished work of art up because when I think on it, I recall the stunning description of this urn. Although an urn is, for all intents and purposes, just a vase, Keats carefully provides the reader with a buffet for the senses. It would be lovely if women were described the way Keats wove words together so beautifully to characterize the urn. Below are some women, both historical figures and personal acquaintances that have motivated and enlightened me. The common thread is they have all done something great with their lives. No matter their circumstances, these women have inspired me to be a better woman, strive for greatness and never think I am anything less than I truly am. I dedicate this chapter to them and their accomplishments.

ADA LOVELACE

Born in 1815, Augusta Ada Byron was a mathematician, writer and a lady of British aristocracy. Who says you can't have brains and beauty, right? The daughter of Lord Byron and his wife, Anne Isabella, Ada was a beauty who not only was well-known in high society for her wit and gambling, but also for her bright mind. As a child, her mother was concerned about Ada taking on her father's eccentricities and so, she raised her on a strict diet of science, math and logic. Ada had a female scientific mentor named Mary Sommerville, who introduced her to Charles Babbage. In a time when women were practically nonexistent in the field of science, Ada assisted Mr. Babbage in creating one of the ideas for a modern-day computer, known as The Analytical Engine. Though the machine was never built, her notes contained the first computer algorithm, which was eventually used by Alan Turing, in the 1940s, to build one of the first modern computers. Because her brilliant work was ahead of the curve, we can now thank the Lady Lovelace every time we log on to our *Instagram* or *Facebook* accounts. Ada tragically died of uterine cancer at the young age of 36, leaving behind a technological legacy that would prove worthy of the future's brightest minds.

JUDITH JAMISON

Growing up in a dance family, I knew of Judith Jamison and her work with the *Alvin Ailey American Dance Theater*, but it's only as an adult that I've realized how much of an impact she made on my youth as a dancer. Judith is as stunning today as she was then; an artistic goddess with fire in her eyes and power radiating through her being. She has the type of warm smile that will win over anyone. Judith was raised in Philadelphia during the 1940's and 50's and was lucky enough to be trained as a child in dance, as well as piano and violin. At 17, she entered Fisk University, where she studied dance technique, kinesiology and Labanotation (a system of movement notation). Her studies led Judith to New York City in 1964, at the behest of Agnes de Mille, who was choreographing a piece on the famed *American Ballet Theater.*

Ms. de Mille recognized Judith's unique talents, and wanted to give her a role in the piece. It is in New York that Ms. Jamison began her work with Alvin Ailey and his dance company. Through the years, Judith has danced and choreographed all over the world. She has had her own dance troupe, The Jamison Project, and even became artistic director of Alvin Ailey American Dance Theater in 1989. Since then, the company and its repertory have flourished, while the school has expanded immensely and given opportunities to thousands of young dancers of every ethnicity from all over the world. Ms. Jamison even wrote an autobiography entitled *Dancing Spirit*, which was edited by Jacqueline Kennedy Onassis.

She has been the recipient of countless awards and was even an inductee into the Hall of Fame at the National Museum of Dance. The accolades go on and on for this muse of dance, but one stands out in particular. Judith is well known for her famed solo, *Cry*, choreographed by Ailey himself and originally dedicated to his mother. The piece is about the hardships and sorrows so many women of color faced and eventually overcame. *Cry* is a celebration of choreography; it is while watching this piece that I first saw the power of what a strong female dancer could do with herself and a stage. The emotions that ran through Judith were so palpable, the moves so gut wrenching, I couldn't look away. To this day, Ms. Jamison works tirelessly to protect and share the legacy of Mr. Ailey's work. She is a true artist and gift to the dance world.

NELL SHIPMAN

Born Helen Foster-Barham in 1892, "Nell" was an actress, director, producer, screenwriter and animal-rights activist. Based out of the Pacific Northwest, Nell had her own production company called *Shipman-Curwood Producing Company* and was definitely a pioneer for women in the film industry. *Shipman* was her first husband's last name. Ernie Shipman was an actor and businessman who helped get financing for her early films. During her career, Nell created over fifteen films, many of them outdoor adventures. She would write, produce, direct, star in and edit all of her projects.

She was an all-around woman who was very much about writing feminist heroines into her films, which at the time was often seen as controversial. Nell was also known for housing a menagerie of 200 wild animals that she would use in her films, but eventually had to give them up to the San Diego Zoo because her company went bankrupt. Nell was married twice and her son,

Barry, became a writer for shows such as *Dick Tracy* and *The Lone Ranger*. For a young woman like myself in the entertainment industry today, I feel it's important to remember the women that came before me and their struggles to get the job done and the film made, no matter the opposition. In her time, Nell was a popular name in the industry. Like many women with projects in today's movie world, lack of funding was a huge roadblock to her company's success. Through many challenges though, Nell continued to persevere till her dying day and I am forever grateful that a trail-blazing woman like her existed.

ROSE VINCENT

When I think of a badass, Southern Belle turned wild, western woman, I think of my dear friend Rose Vincent. Rose is a family friend who, from the first moment we met, has shown me nothing but love and support for my art, my business and myself.

Born in North Carolina to a middle class family with four children, Rose grew up with a dark-skinned maid named Elsie, a businessman father and a mother who spent her afternoons drinking too much and playing tennis at the local country club. "North Carolina is about as southern as southern gets. The joke is that people there are still talking about the war, The Civil War of course;

you aren't southern if you have to ask which one." As a young girl, Rose was expected to look pretty, have impeccable manners, be a debutante and marry a nice lawyer or doctor so that she could continue her life at the country club. "Man, was I an unexpected deviation from the norm!" When she was fourteen, in 1968, she discovered a whole new world at the local college. With long haired-artists, live music and the counter culture in full swing, Rose absolutely loved it. She immediately doubled up on her high school work and made it into a college honors program for law school when she was only 16. A year later, after dropping out of law school, Rose married a young Italian guitar player in Florida and quickly discovered how life is when you are young, married and broke. She ended up working for a plant nursery alongside migrant farm workers who picked oranges. She had "the uptown job" though, sitting on a bucket all day long, pulling weeds out of plants in nursery pots laid out in a three-acre plot. After a year or so, Rose's husband had an affair with a local girl. Once she found out, she drove all the way back to North Carolina, furious and heartbroken, but determined.

"I lost my innocence about believing guys should take care of you; so I knew that hell or high water from then on, I was going to take care of myself." The following year, her father was diagnosed with cancer, and

Chapter Eleven

her mother's drinking became more than a problem. "My daddy was my hero and before he died, he suggested I move far, far away and that's how I got to Austin, TX. I looked at a map, spotted Austin and thought, wow, I've heard there are hippies, music and cowboys there, sounds good!" Going from a country club social scene where everyone knows your family to never seeing one familiar face tested all of Rose's courage. She was alone, broke and waitressing at Willie Nelson's bar just to get by. "I turned twenty-one celebrating my birthday by eating sardines and crackers on the hood of my car in front of the ugliest apartment on the planet. Alone." Rose pushed through that time with a strong determination, working 12 hour days, waitressing and managing a few plant contracts at a couple of downtown office buildings. As tough as it was, she owned her future and her dreams were beginning to come true.

At 27, Rose met Ross and instantly knew that this charming, artistic, Maine-woods guy was the man for her. They dated for eight months before getting married and spent 32 happy years together. They created a beautiful family and a thriving business before Ross passed away from cancer three years ago. This left Rose once more in a new phase of life. "I have spent the last couple years trying to remember exactly who I used to be and now, who I am. I want to be the unstoppable, courageous girl sitting on the hood of my car on my 21st birthday. From pulling weeds to creating vistas for multimillion-dollar properties, it has been a ride, but I knew I could make it happen if I just wanted it bad enough. The best gift I have been given is to know those goals of a 21-year-old woman are still very much alive and well in this 61-year-old grandmother!"

AUNT BEA

"My men never strayed, they just died." Truer words have never been spoken when it comes to the great Beatrice Gordon Aronowitz Stein Harris (yes, she has been married once or twice). The seventh of eight children, my grandmother's Aunt Bea, was born in 1913 and is still kicking today at the whopping age of 103. This woman has definitely experienced a lot in her life. She was born before both World Wars, before women earned the right to vote, one year after the Titanic sank and the same year Harriet Tubman died. Aunt Bea has survived three marriages, birthed three children, and then lost one to suicide. She has lived through the depression, a double mastectomy and is now experiencing dementia, but through all this, Bea has never once lost her spunk. "Why bother wasting life because of your hardships?" Can you imagine growing up in a Harlem walk-up tenement, without a phone or running hot water and living all the

Chapter Eleven

way to an era where we have touch screen Iphones, Ipads, androids and talking robots?! It's crazy.

At one point, Aunt Bea owned her own bowling alley in Brooklyn on the corner Kings Highway and Coney Island Ave. Her business thrived for over 15 years, attracting all sorts of crowds from tourists and locals to the mafia. The Mob bosses would arrive at closing, ask for the doors to be locked, unholstered their guns and enjoyed a few rounds on the house. Aunt Bea was not stupid. What I admire most about my great-grandmother's sister (and why I feel she should be recognized) is that as long as she's been around, she has always believed age is only a state of mind. Bea will tell you today that she feels 70 not 103. Thanks to good genes and Pond's cold cream; her skin looks as youthful as ever. She loves to dance and gamble and still wants me to paint her nails and do her makeup every time I visit. Though her mind is not what it once was, Aunt Bea can remember the most remarkable details of her childhood. She is a truly exceptional woman and when asked about her dating advice, Aunt Bea simply remarked, "A woman should always keep her man psychologically interested, that way, he won't stray."

*My Aunt Bea passed away a week after I finished the first draft of this book. I'm sure she would have been proud to read it and know her great-grandniece was creating content for women. She left behind a beautiful legacy and has been laid to rest in Florida.

JESSICA LIZAMA

Born and raised an army brat, Jessica is no stranger to tough times. Growing up the oldest of three siblings, her dad was a drill sergeant in the Army and her mother worked to help support the family, relocating every two to three years all over the country. With this type of childhood, Jess had to learn to start over and make new friends quickly, a skill she has definitely carried over into her adult life. After having a child at 16 and struggling as a single mother, Jess got started a new media in 2009, with the launch of her *YouTube* channel, *ExoticJess;* *"*Exotic like a flower of course, being that I'm Chamorro and Irish.*"* Early on, Jess realized that she was constantly needing to explain where her channel name came from, and she also noticed that "mom brands" were turning her away. It was then that she decided it was time for a change. Jess took a risk and a huge hit in viewers, because not all of her sketch comedy audience members were interested exclusively in beauty videos and mom reviews. "I think as women in this space, especially when you're comedy-centered, you're put into a tiny box and expected to perform at an extraordinary pace. You know, keep up with the men, but maintain your femininity and remain delicate. What the hell does that even look like?!" Jess stayed true to herself and today she is a proud entrepreneur who creates the content that she wants and is able to support her family, live spontaneously and still tuck something away for her daughter.

Though *YouTube* completely changed her life, most of her finances are generated from her brand: a website, e-commerce and sponsorships. "I tell my daughter all the time to follow her dreams and go with her gut! Live fearlessly, love passionately and don't give a flying shit flame what anyone else thinks! If you live by some variation of that phrase, you'll be just fine!" I'm in awe of Jess because after all she has been through, she's still such a kind, young woman who is immensely driven and real. She is a beautiful soul who lights up a room. I admire her personality and from her I have learned that our pasts don't always have to define our futures.

In conclusion, wherever your journey may take you in this life, no one can judge you, but you. As long as you're not hurting yourself or others, do whatever you must do in good conscience, to have the life you want. When the goal is survival, people can become quite amazing. Any woman who pushes herself and achieves her dreams is winning in my book. My grandma always tells me to be aware and keep an eye towards the future.

Make sure you take care of *you* first and foremost. Family, marriage, friend, children, riches, and the good life, all mean nothing if you are not around to enjoy what you have built.

Final Musings

If eyes are the windows to the soul, then let them shine. I recommend spending time looking at yourself in the mirror and be clear about what you want your eyes to portray when you go out into the world; happiness, mystery, seduction, power, etc.

Be grateful for what you have been given, the good and the bad. The good for what it has brought you and the bad for what it taught you. A lady should take time now and again to reflect on what has occurred in her life and what she has to look forward to in her future. It took me many years to grasp the concept of truly having gratitude for my being and my existence. This idea is not a hippie thing or new age crap. Gratitude is straight up energetically healthy and gives you a sexy glow of calm confidence. Whether your successes are self-made or given, be grateful from your core and be humble. It makes you more beautiful inside and out. This is not to say be timid and don't take credit for your accomplishments. By all means, wave that flag of success, but do it with finesse. Don't cut others down and act like a damn fool. Your success is about you and you alone. What you have achieved in life (and what you may still be working on) is what you have brought to yourself. Whether consciously creating, energetically manifesting, or spilling your own blood, sweat and tears, your achievements count, no matter how small or large.

Chapter Eleven

Compromise when you need to, but never let anyone, of either sex, dictate what you should or should not be doing as you age. Everyone has their own journey to take and it is very important not to compare your own struggles to another's. Every person on this planet is different and they will have their own path, so stick to the one you are laying out for yourself.

My mom always says to me, "It takes a village," meaning that when you achieve greatness in your accomplishments, there are, more often than not, always others to thank who helped you get there. Don't forget your supporters, the ones who gave you your first opportunities or believed in you when no one else did. Don't ever forget them! Sara Blakely, (look her up!) Oprah, Madonna, or any other diva for that matter, are not where they are today simply because they are talented or had a great idea. These moguls have an entire team behind them, helping every step of the way. Their "village" often consists of family members or close friends, but those are the ones that have been with you since day one and knew who you were back in the day. Don't leave behind those who helped you in the beginning when you were a nobody, but certainly don't forget the people who hindered you from getting what you wanted either. Those sly snakes will eventually creep back into your life once you have achieved greatness. They will feign kindness and act like nothing hurtful ever happened between you. Often, they will even go as far as to say *they* were the ones who got you there.

It causes me great distress when I see women seeming to forget what these people did to them and continuing to be friends. It's not always healthy or beneficial to have those people around you and, chances are, if they hindered you once, it will happen again.

Allow your disposition to be one of confidence, consideration, strength and kindness. I pray that this book gives you even one fresh thought, idea or tip on assisting yourself to be greater every day. Despite setbacks, women of all backgrounds, throughout history, have been through the fire. Yet, we continue to fight, succeed and flourish. So, ladies, do right by the females that came before you. Learn from them, teach our youth, stand proud, and don't take shit from those that would see you fail with pleasure.

IN CONCLUSION...

You're never going to get life perfect, because there will always be something more that you want or are working towards. To be a woman is to be strong of will and heart as well as understanding with yourself. When you kiss, do it with passion and intention. When you love, love strong and certain. Be who you want and live honestly to the core. As a woman, know that you are a lucky and blessed individual. So, go forth knowing that though you are continually evolving, somewhere deep inside you lies the female, the queen, the bearer of life, and one hell of a stunning creature.

Take the crown that is your birthright and always wear it with immense pride, love and the knowledge that you are the art that creates the woman.

ACKNOWLEDGEMENT

My sincerest gratitude goes to everyone who answered my questions and gave their time to this book. You know who you are. Thank you! Thank you!

Special thanks to:

-G. Santini- who is one hell of a scholar and gentleman. Without you, this book might not ever have been.

-Trish… you have been such an amazing angel through this process. All of your assistance helped bring this book to life. I love you and appreciate your belief in both my work and myself.

-Rob G. and Jess L. for all of your wonderful help in the creation process when I had no idea what I was doing.

- Thank you to my beautiful fitness model Vania!

-My beautiful sister Chelsea. You are my world, my spiritual twin and my light. Without you, I am nothing.

Acknowledgement

You are the greatest thing this universe has ever given me, Baby Bird.

-Tray Tray, you are my best friend, confidant and ride or die. I'm TRULY blessed to have you in this fight to the top. Keep rocking those sunglasses, and thank you for being my tanager.

-To both my parents, thank you for creating me and supporting me while I follow each and every crazy dream. Love you always.

For more information on some of the badass women who helped to contribute:

Carolyn Hennesy: carolynhennesy.com

Jessica Lizama: youtube.com/jess_lizama

Natalia Fedner: NataliaFednerDesign.com

(IG/ Twitter) @nataliafedner

BIBLIOGRAPHY

Fairley, Josephine, and Lorna McKay. ***The Perfume Bible.*** London: Kyle, 2014. Print.

Curtis, Tony, and David G. Williams. ***Introduction to Perfumery.*** Port Washington, NY: Micelle, 2001. Print.

Thorpe, JR. ***"The Strange History of Perfume, From Ancient Roman Foot Fragrance to Napoleon's Cologne."*** Bustle. Bustle, 31 July 2015. Web. 24 Dec. 2016.

"**Etiquette**." *Wikipedia.* Wikimedia Foundation, 07 May 2017. Web. 17 March 2016.

Sink, Nancy. "**Women's Liberation Movement.**" *Women's Liberation Movement.* N.p., Dec. 2008. Web. 09 Aug. 2016.

"**Timeline of the Women's Liberation Movement.**" *The British Library*. The British Library, 06 May 2014. Web. 11 Aug. 2016.

Brownmiller, Susan. *Against Our Will: Men, Women and Rape*. New York: Fawcett, 2010. Print.

"**Causes: The Woman Suffrage Movement**." *Women in the Progressive Era*. National Women's History Museum, n.d. Web. 11 Aug. 2016.

Armatage, Kay. *The Girl From God's Country: Nell Shipman and the Silent Cinema*. Toronto: U of Toronto, 2003. Print.

Jamison, Judith, and Howard Kaplan. *Dancing Spirit: An Autobiography.* New York: Anchor, 1994. Print.

"**Ada Lovelace**." *Wikipedia*. Wikimedia Foundation, 06 May 2017. Web. 21 Feb. 2016.

"**Ada Lovelace**." *Babbage Engine | Computer History Museum*. Computer History Museum, n.d. Web. 21 Feb. 2016.

Weed, Susun S. *Breast Cancer? Breast Health!: The Wise Woman Way*. Woodstock, NY: Ash Tree Pub., 1996. Print.

www.ingramcontent.com/pod-product-compliance
Lightning Source LLC
Chambersburg PA
CBHW040334300426
44113CB00021B/2747